THE
PROSPERITY OF
THE WICKED

A STUDY OF PSALM 73

Jim Osman

Kootenai Community Church Publishing
Kootenai, Idaho

<u>Other Books by Jim Osman</u>

Truth or Territory:
A Biblical Approach to Spiritual Warfare

Selling the Stairway to Heaven:
Critiquing the Claims of Heaven Tourists

The Prosperity of the Wicked: A Study of Psalm 73

Dedication

This book is dedicated to the loving, joy-filled, faithful saints that gather as Kootenai Community Church, who make it a joy to serve as an undershepherd of Jesus Christ.

The Prosperity of the Wicked: A Study of Psalm 73

Note to the Reader

Thank you for buying this book! I pray this will be well worth the sacrifice of time and money. It probably will be. After all, it's only time, and it's only money. The time will pass whether you read this or not, and you can't take the money with you. Speaking of the money, you should know that ALL the proceeds from the sale of this book (as well as my other books) go to the building fund of Kootenai Community Church. Since 2002 we have been meeting in a rented facility while we work on constructing a new church building to house our worship and ministry. We have committed to do this debt-free and it has been a long process (it is currently 2016). We have trusted in God for His provision and He has graciously given to us what we need when we need it. Though it is a sacrifice to set up and clean up every weekend, the believers at Kootenai have been faithful and flexible through it all. Even after we move into our new building there will be work that needs to be done to finish the construction. So, for as long as I am alive, the proceeds from my books will go to the construction of our facility. After I die, they will go to my wife and children. If you ever hear that I have died, please go out and buy another copy of this book. Do it for the children! ☺

The Prosperity of the Wicked: A Study of Psalm 73

Table of Contents

The Prosperity of the Wicked: A Study of Psalm 73

Acknowledgements

I never skip the acknowledgments in any book I read. Usually I can tell from the first couple of lines if the author will merely provide a boring and unimaginative list of people who had some hand in the work, or if he will thoughtfully, engagingly, and sometimes humorously give some credit where it is due. I could opt for the former, but that really wouldn't be my style. So, I hope this provides the latter.

First, I want to thank you, dear reader, for buying this book and taking the time to read it. I know it is a sacrifice of valuable time and resources and I pray that it may be richly rewarded by the pages that follow.

There are a few folks who have had a direct hand in the production of this book without whose help, in various ways, my work would be greatly increased. My thanks to Jenny Leo who graciously took time to edit these chapters before they first appeared in the newsletter of Kootenai Community Church. My secretary, Marcia Whetsel, works diligently to keep non-essential work off my desk and out of my ever-diminishing amount of hair so that I have a bit of time each week to work on writing. Without her diligent service, I would be continually buried in distractions and frustrations. Kootenai Church is blessed with a lot of creative and technical talent. Josh Comstock is among those blessings. He is the designer responsible for the cover art.

I continue to be blessed by the saints that gather as Kootenai Community Church. Their love, support, and encouragement are used by God in my own sanctification and growth. They joyfully look forward to every break in my preaching I take for writing. The three week break from the discouragement of Ecclesiastes that I took to finish this book was received with enthusiastic exuberance. It is a great blessing to serve this incredibly mature and gifted body of believers. Thank you, all!

My fellow elders, Cornel Rasor, Dave Rich, and Jess Whetsel, only increase the joy of serving the saints at Kootenai Community Church. Their friendship, fellowship, and faithfulness to the truth inspire and humble me. They are not just peers; they are friends, and dear ones at that. Their faithfulness to Christ is an example to all they lead and serve. May God grant us many years of service together!

Every day of my life proves true the words of Proverbs 18:22: "He who finds a wife finds a good thing and obtains favor from the LORD." I happen to have one who is excellent and whose worth is far above jewels (Proverbs 31:10). Her contribution to the quality of this book is immeasurable. With love, skill, and dedication she has pored over every word on these pages, not once, not twice, but four separate times to ensure that the book you hold in your hand is readable. She checks my spelling, my grammar, and my tone in a continual effort to keep everyone from realizing she married a clown. Trust me, it is a continual effort. One of these days, the secret will come out.

Last, but certainly not least, I gladly thank the One who has lavished me with untold, undeserved blessings. I thank the God and Father of our Lord Jesus Christ for saving, sanctifying, and securing me until the very end. "I know Whom I have believed and I am confident that He is able to keep what I have committed to Him until that great day" (2 Timothy 1:12). Jesus Christ is "the blessed and only Sovereign, the King of kings and Lord of lords, who alone possesses immortality and dwells in unapproachable light, whom no man has seen or can see. To Him be honor and eternal dominion! Amen" (1 Timothy 6:15–16).

Soli Deo Gloria!

Preface

The prosperity of the wicked is a perplexing dilemma for the righteous in every age. The Bible provides the answer to this dilemma in clear and convincing terms.

Our distress over the success of the wicked and the suffering of the righteous is due entirely to a wrong perspective. If we do not have the same perspective on prosperity that God does, we will wonder why it is that those who hate Him appear to receive the most of His blessing. It is only when we enter the sanctuary of God that we gain the understanding necessary to rightly assess this seeming inequity. To answer this riddle, God does not change the circumstances. He changes our understanding of the circumstances. It is this change of perspective that moved Asaph out of his gut-wrenching crisis of faith and into confident trust in God's goodness to those who are His. In this book, you will journey with Asaph from his crisis of faith through the sanctuary of God and into a confident felicity.

The structure of this book follows closely the outline of Psalm 73.

Part 1 covers the text of Psalm 73:1-14, looking at The Perplexing Problem of Prosperity as Asaph saw and experienced it. Chapters 1-5 look at the wicked in all their glory and affluence. The inequities of life in this world are described in all their frustrating detail. We will look at the soul-crushing realities that so vexed Asaph.

Part 2 examines Psalm 73:15-28 and explains The Proper Perspective on the Prosperous as Asaph gained a God-centered view on the prosperity of the wicked. In chapters 4-6 we will see the "end" for both the wicked and the righteous. It is an "end" that explains all inequities.

Along the way we will tackle a few issues connected to the text: the justice of God, the meaning of prosperity, the reality of Hell, and others. Psalm 73 provides abundant encouragement to the child of God in today's world. Let us join Asaph in the sanctuary of God and learn of His goodness to those who are pure in heart.

Psalm 73:1: "Surely God is good to Israel, to those who are pure in heart!"

Soli Deo Gloria!

Introduction:
A Significant Psalm

Why do the wicked prosper? We have all wondered it. Our questions about this great inequity of life come in many forms. Our frustrations find many different expressions. Mankind may be separated by language, culture, politics, skin color, or borders, but one thing unites us all: we have all known the frustration of watching the wicked prosper.

Seeing evil people do evil things is not unique to any one culture. Neither is seeing evil people who do evil things and getting away with it. Equally universal is seeing evil people do evil things and not only getting away with it, but prospering in and from their evil.

Sometimes it comes in innocuous and annoying but otherwise trivial forms, like watching your favorite sports team get fouled at a critical point in the game. Insult is added to injury as you watch the injustice played over and over in slow motion from every conceivable angle, while even the "unbiased" commentators acknowledge the refs missed a crucial call. When the offending team gains an advantage and goes on to win the game, arguably due to that missed penalty, you cannot help but feel that a great injustice has ripped apart the fabric of the space-time continuum—at least until your team gets away with an equal or greater injustice.

I have noticed this among sports enthusiasts: we tend not to view injustices that benefit us with the same moral indignation as those that benefit others. I have watched enough football games with friends whose favorite team is opposite my own to observe this—most certainly in myself. I have yet to see anyone stand up, shout at the TV, and cry foul when their favorite team "got away with one." That is probably why I love sports: it brings out the best in us and the worst in us.

The injustice and moral wrong of a cheating team or player is inconsequential when compared to the grander injustices of life. When a tyrannical dictator rules his country with an iron fist, stamping out all dissent, freedom, and even the will to live, we are rightly incensed. When we see the ruler of North Korea murder his political opponents, starve his people, commit genocide, rape women, and abuse children, we get a glimpse at real injustice, real wickedness. When we see such men prosper from those actions, our moral sensitivities are inflamed.

Compared to a dictator starving children while he lives in unimaginable wealth, the cheating NFL cornerback who steals the game is pretty mild. Guess which one we spend our time talking about?

Prospering Through the Ages

Why do the wicked prosper? Examples abound. You can list plenty. I can list plenty. I will include a number of such examples in this book.

Examples abound not just in our own day but all through human history. If you were to travel back through time to any era of human history, you would find not only that wicked men and women appear to prosper in their wickedness, but you would find righteous men and women asking the question, "Why is this so?"

Job had every reason to wonder why the wicked prospered. He was "blameless, upright, fearing God and turning away from evil" (Job 1:1).[1] God said to Satan, "Have you considered My servant Job? For there is no one like him on the earth, a blameless and upright man, fearing God and turning away from evil" (1:8). Job was notable from among all men for His holiness and piety.

Yet Job suffered the loss of all things. By the sovereign hand of God, Job lost his livestock (1:13-17), his children (1:18-19), and his own health and comfort (2:7-9) in rapid succession. To make matters worse, his own wife failed to be of any comfort or consolation (1:9-10) and the three friends who arrived to console him only rubbed salt in his wounds by accusing Job of all kinds of hideous secret sins. Job's experience appeared to be an enormous cosmic injustice.

Job observed that while he, a righteous man, suffered, the wicked did not. In fact, the wicked were secure and prospered. Further, it seemed as if their security and prosperity were the blessing of God upon them.

Job 12:5-6:
5 He who is at ease holds calamity in contempt,
    As prepared for those whose feet slip.
6 The tents of the destroyers prosper,
    And those who provoke God are secure,
    Whom God brings into their power.

What could be any more unjust than Job's suffering compared to the security and prosperity of those who provoked God?

---

1. Scripture taken from the *NEW AMERICAN STANDARD BIBLE* ®, Copyright © 1960, 1962, 1963, 1968, 1971, 1972, 1973, 1975, 1977, 1995 by The Lockman Foundation. Used by permission. www.Lockman.org.

Job returned to this theme in Chapter 21 in response to Zophar's claim that "the triumphing of the wicked is short, and the joy of the godless momentary" (20:5). Zophar claimed of the wicked: "His prosperity does not endure.... This is the wicked man's portion from God, even the heritage decreed to him by God" (20:21, 29). *woops – not quite right –*

Zophar's point could hardly be missed. He was claiming that in this life, the wicked receive what they are due and the righteous are blessed by God. Since Job was suffering some of the very things that Zophar claimed came upon the wicked, the implication was obvious: Job was suffering because of his sin.

Job countered by pointing out that this seldom happens the way that Zophar claimed.

I TIM 4:16 – Keep a close watch on how you live and on your teaching.

Job 21:7–13:

7 Why do the wicked still live,
  Continue on, also become very powerful?
8 Their descendants are established with them in their sight,
  And their offspring before their eyes,
9 Their houses are safe from fear,
  And the rod of God is not on them.
10 His ox mates without fail;
  His cow calves and does not abort.
11 They send forth their little ones like the flock,
  And their children skip about.
12 They sing to the timbrel and harp
  And rejoice at the sound of the flute.
13 They spend their days in prosperity,
  And suddenly they go down to Sheol.

That hardly sounds like a rough life! It seems the wicked enjoy all sorts of blessings, comforts, and joys. Do the wicked lose their livestock, their livelihood, and their children all in one day?

No. Their livestock prospers. Their descendants are established before their eyes. They don't end their life in intense suffering like Job was enduring. Instead, their death is sudden and swift as they are plucked from the lap of luxury without suffering or loss. And that is not all!

Job 21:14–16:

14 They say to God, "Depart from us!
   We do not even desire the knowledge of Your ways.
15 Who is the Almighty, that we should serve Him,
   And what would we gain if we entreat Him?"
16 Behold, their prosperity is not in their hand;
   The counsel of the wicked is far from me.

All the prosperity that the wicked enjoyed, they enjoyed in spite of their open rebellion against God, His truth, and His ways. The wicked men whom Job described saw no benefit to knowing God or serving Him. When he said that "their prosperity is not in their hand," he meant that it was God who had given them that prosperity. Ultimately, Job knew that God was the One Who gave all things to all men. If any man, including the wicked, enjoyed any earthly good, it was by God's hand.

Job 21:17-20:

17 How often is the lamp of the wicked put out,
   Or does their calamity fall on them?
   Does God apportion destruction in His anger?
18 Are they as straw before the wind,
   And like chaff which the storm carries away?
19 You say, "God stores away a man's iniquity for his sons."
   Let God repay him so that he may know it.
20 Let his own eyes see his decay,
   And let him drink of the wrath of the Almighty.

5

test your doctrinal assertions Biblically

Those questions directly challenged Zophar's assertion that the "triumphing of the wicked is short."

"Really?" asked Job. "How often is the lamp of the wicked put out? Does calamity fall on them? Do they really experience the wrath of God for their sin?" Zophar may answer that God will punish their children in His wrath (v. 19), but is that really any consolation? Wouldn't it be more just if God should repay the wicked themselves that they might know God's justice?

Job's observations sound as contemporary as this morning's headlines.

Habakkuk and Jeremiah

The Old Testament Prophet, Habakkuk, wrestled with the same quandary. He expressed his righteous indignation over the sin in the land and cried out to God to deal with the wicked, saying in Habakkuk 1:2-4:

> 2 How long, O Lord, will I call for help,
>   And You will not hear?
> I cry out to You, "Violence!"
>   Yet You do not save.
> 3 Why do You make me see iniquity,
>   And cause me to look on wickedness?
> Yes, destruction and violence are before me;
>   Strife exists and contention arises.
> 4 Therefore the law is ignored
>   And justice is never upheld.
> For the wicked surround the righteous;
>   Therefore justice comes out perverted.

God informed Habakkuk that in spite of appearances, He was, in fact, going to judge the sin that Habakkuk lamented. God was raising up the Babylonian nation for that very purpose. They would be God's chosen instrument to bring judgment upon the disobedient nation. This only added to Habakkuk's problem since the Chaldeans were even more wicked than Israel. How could God judge wicked Israel with a nation even more wicked?

Habakkuk 1:13–17:
13 Your eyes are too pure to approve evil,
    And You cannot look on wickedness with favor.
Why do You look with favor
    On those who deal treacherously?
Why are You silent when the wicked swallow up
    Those more righteous than they?

How could God allow an even more wicked nation to triumph over His own people? Sure Israel was sinful, but the Chaldeans?! The Chaldeans were a godless and idolatrous people who gave praise to their false gods for all their military triumphs and the abundant wealth they enjoyed (1:14-17). They made the most wicked of Jews look like pious choir boys by comparison.

Habakkuk was wrestling with this very same issue: why do the wicked (Chaldeans) prosper? For Habakkuk it was personal since the prospering of the Chaldeans would come at his expense and the expense of people he cared about.

Jeremiah faced the same Chaldean invasion that Habakkuk described. Jeremiah said:

Righteous are You, O Lord, that I would plead my case with You; indeed I would discuss matters of justice with You: why has the way of the wicked prospered? Why are all those who deal in treachery at ease? (Jeremiah 12:1)

These men have put words to the thoughts many of us have had. Watching wicked men prosper while the righteous suffer affliction is vexing to the righteous. These perplexing questions

lying politicians killing millions of people in the womb and out of the womb. False teachers leading those desiring to go to hell.

have been raised by men on every continent, in every culture, and through every century. It is enough to make even the most righteous believer question the justice of God's dealings with men.

Getting God's Perspective

The Bible not only raises these questions but answers them as well. God has given us His perspective on the prosperity of the wicked. There is one particular passage that is the focus of this book – Psalm 73.

The Bible has plenty to say on the subject of money, wealth, and prosperity. The Bible also has plenty to say on the subject of suffering and affliction. God has revealed the truth regarding the wicked and their ultimate end. Psalm 73 brings all the teachings of Scripture on these topics into sharp focus. God has not left us in the dark concerning these perplexing issues. He has given us His perspective. *and He never does. why walk crooked?*

ALWAYS TRUE Left to our own devices, we could never solve this puzzling problem. Human wisdom and human reason alone could never adequately understand this seemingly great inequity. We could never figure out why those who sin and flout God's law prosper in their rebellion, and why those who love and serve God seem to suffer and go without. Left to our own understanding, we would never understand why the easy life falls to the children of Satan and the difficult life falls to God's child. Who would be sufficient for these things?

study diligently We need revelation. We need God to answer this, and He has. When we get God's perspective, we will see the abundant prosperity of the wicked for what it really is. We will not envy it. We will not wish it on ourselves. When we get God's perspective we will be able to affirm, "God is good to Israel, to those who are pure in heart" (Psalm 73:1).

Introducing Psalm 73

The rest of this book is going to be an exposition of the 73rd Psalm. Don't let the term "exposition" scare you off. This simply means I will be "exposing" the text to you by explaining the meaning and application of this very important psalm.

I have divided the psalm into its various thematic sections. Each chapter will progressively explain and apply those sections.

This book is the product of two sermons I preached on Psalm 73 in May of 2014. I found the teaching and theology of this psalm so rich that I struggled to keep it to only two sermons.[2] So much rich material hit the editing-room floor of my sermon prep that I determined to write a book on the psalm. This psalm is so profound, I could not leave it alone.

Since all that is to follow is an exposition of the psalm, it will be helpful if we have a brief introduction to the psalm, its author, theme, and outline.

The Author

Psalm 73 begins with these words: "A Psalm of Asaph." You will find those in your Bible prior to verse 1. That is not a notation added by your Bible translators. Those introductory comments are actually part of the inspired text of the psalm. Some introductions are longer than others and often provide information helpful in properly interpreting the psalm.

For instance, Psalm 57 begins: "For the choir director; set to Al-tashheth. A Miktam of David, when he fled from Saul in the cave." Those words help us understand the historical setting in which the psalm was written and provide valuable insight into David's emotional state at the time.

---

2. Those two messages are available at http://kootenaichurch.org/kcc-audio/special-messages/

9

All we are told at the beginning of Psalm 73 is that this is "A Psalm of Asaph." We need to look entirely outside this psalm to discover who Asaph was.

The Asaph who is the author of this psalm is the very same Asaph who was a contemporary of King David. Asaph was a Levite appointed by King David to lead Israel in singing "with instruments of music, harps, lyres, [and] loud-sounding cymbals" to "raise sounds of joy" (1 Chronicles 15:16-17, 19). This singing and praise was to accompany the transportation of the Ark of the Covenant from the house of Obed-edom to the place that David had prepared for it (1 Chronicles 15:1, 25).

Asaph was then selected as a chief musician (1 Chronicles 16:4-5) to lead the celebration and praise before the Ark of God (1 Chronicles 16:4, 7).

Asaph was apparently a very gifted musician. He distinguished himself enough that he and his relatives were appointed by David himself. Hundreds of years later, the "sons of Asaph" were still among those Levites who were fulfilling the musical office assigned to their great ancestor (Ezra 2:41; 3:10; Nehemiah 7:44; 11:17, 22; 12:35-36).

In 2 Chronicles 29:30 he is referred to as "Asaph the seer." This indicates there was a sense in which Asaph was recognized to be a man with some degree of prophetic function. He was a channel of divine revelation, some of which is recorded in the psalms that bear his name.

Asaph's musical and theological giftedness is plainly evident in the psalms he authored. There are twelve psalms that bear his name. Psalm 50 is the first psalm we encounter written by Asaph. The rest of his psalms are clustered together with Psalm 73 standing at the head of eleven consecutive psalms (Psalms 73-83).

Reading through the twelve psalms he wrote gives us a feel for the rich theological depth of this great man of God. As David Engelsma writes, "A reading of these psalms shows that Asaph had a lively sense of the warfare of the people of God with the ungodly and a profound awareness of the suffering and struggles of the saints in this life."[3] For certain, Asaph understood the struggles of life in this fallen world. He shares with us some of those struggles in Psalm 73.

The Theme

Psalm 73 recounts a personal, private, and intimate struggle of faith that Asaph experienced. There was a time when Asaph saw the prosperity of the wicked and he envied their position (v. 3). He confesses that he was "envious of the arrogant."

For a time, Asaph struggled to affirm that God was good to Israel. He was perplexed by what he saw (v. 16). It did not seem right that those who were pure in heart were afflicted and chastened (vv. 13-14) while the wicked lived a life of ease and increasing wealth (v. 12).

Being a righteous man, Asaph struggled to understand why his righteousness did not translate into tangible earthly blessings like those enjoyed by evil men. Wasn't God pleased with his holiness? Shouldn't God have blessed those who pursued holiness and moral purity? Why would His blessings rest on those who gave no thought to God or His law (v. 11)?

Thinking through these realities was troubling to Asaph - so much so, he confessed that at one point he doubted God's goodness to those who are His. Verse 2: "But as for me, my feet

---

3 David J. Engelsma, *Prosperous Wicked and Plagued Saints: An Exposition of Psalm 73* (Kindle Locations 95-97). Reformed Free Publishing Association. Kindle Edition.

came close to stumbling, My steps had almost slipped." Asaph tripped over this perplexity and it was nearly his downfall.

His "heart was embittered" and he was "pierced within" (v. 21). This was a crisis of faith in the soul of a godly man. Psalm 73 is the honest account of his struggle.

The Outline

Psalm 73 can be quite cleanly divided into two equal parts. This natural division comes at the end of verse 14, dividing the psalm into two 14-verse sections.

The first 14 verses present us with the perplexing problem of prosperity. The prosperity enjoyed by the wicked is set in stark contrast to the lack of such blessings in the lives of the righteous. The ease of life, abundance of wealth, and comfort in death that is the lot of those who hate God is described with great poetic clarity.

The second half of the psalm gives us the proper perspective on the prosperous. The hinge upon which this psalm turns is in verse 17: "Until I came into the sanctuary of God, then I perceived their end." That truth is the key that unlocks all the riches in this psalm. That is where Asaph gained God's perspective on the lot and life of the wicked. Having God's perspective changed everything for Asaph. Rather than thinking that wealth and ease were his good, Asaph would confess: "The nearness of God is my good" (v. 28). Having God as "the strength of [his] heart and [his] portion forever" was better to Asaph than all the riches and prosperity of the unfaithful (v. 26).

The first half of the psalm is the view of this issue from an earthly perspective. The second half views this issue from Heaven's perspective. The conclusions we would draw from our human reason are contrasted with the conclusions we draw from God's revelation.

So important. Be aware of how you draw your conclusions. Refuse deception in all its forms. Cling to God

The central message of this psalm is that though the prosperity of the wicked may perplex the righteous, that prosperity is short-lived and illusory.

God's Perspective

We desperately need God's perspective on this issue. Every day in our world, the news headlines are filled with the names of wicked men prospering in their wickedness. Our church bulletins and prayer chains are filled with the names of righteous saints suffering affliction.

This will not change. We cannot expect that there will come a time in this age when the wealth of the wicked vanishes and they are saddled with suffering instead. We cannot expect that the affliction of God's people will be suddenly turned to ease of life, earthly comforts, and freedom from pain.

If a Christian does not have God's perspective on this problem, even the most gifted and godly among us can lose heart and become embittered. It is my prayer that the time you spend studying this psalm will equip you to view all of life from God's perspective, establish you in faith that God is good to His people, and encourage you in the confidence that the nearness of God is your good.

Let the faithful of God say with confidence, "I have made the Lord GOD my refuge, that I may tell of all Your works" (Psalm 73:28).

Part 1:

The Perplexing Problem of Prosperity

1

A Truth Affirmed

Psalm 73:1
Surely God is good to Israel,
To those who are pure in heart!

Some people like to know how a story ends before they read the story. I have met people who read the last couple of chapters of a book before they read the book. These same people go online to find out how a movie ends before they watch the movie. They LOVE spoilers! They don't like to be held in suspense. They don't like tension. They want to be assured that everything is going to turn out fine before they read or see anything that suggests otherwise.

These people live among us! They could be your neighbor, your co-worker, or even your babysitter! If this condition afflicts you, please seek biblical ~~professional~~ help immediately!

If you are one who likes to know how the story ends before it starts, you will appreciate Asaph's style in Psalm 73. Asaph begins this psalm with the conclusion of His crisis of faith: "Surely, God is good to Israel, to those who are pure in heart!"

This record of Asaph's internal conflict starts with a positive affirmation of the pure goodness of God. This truth is both the starting point for thinking through the issues raised in this psalm and the conclusion we should reach from a study of the psalm. Confidence in God's goodness permeated Asaph's soul. Though he shared the nature of his own doubts about the goodness of God, he first declared the truth of God's goodness. This truth is an immovable bedrock, an anchor to our soul, and a rock against which our doubts shatter.

What We Know for Sure

The Christian can boldly and joyfully affirm that God is good. We affirm not only that God *is* good, but that God *does* good. In fact, we confidently say that *all* that God does is good because *all* that God *is* is good. "Good" describes God's being - His nature and character. Surely, God is good.

Asaph emphasized the certainty of this truth by beginning the psalm with that short word (composed of only two Hebrew letters) which we translate as "surely." This word is intended to emphasize the certainty of what is to follow. It is the Hebrew Old Testament equivalent of the word "verily" or "truly" that we find in the New Testament.[1]

The goodness of God is not in dispute. God's goodness is an absolute certainty, a rock or refuge for the soul. There are a multitude of things which might be questioned in life, but the goodness of God is not among them. This is the ultimate lesson Asaph learned. This is his conclusion.

---

1. David J. Engelsma, *Prosperous Wicked and Plagued Saints: An Exposition of Psalm 73* (Kindle Location 192). Reformed Free Publishing Association. Kindle Edition. Jesus would often preface important statements with "Truly, truly," to emphasize the certainty and significance of what He was about to say. See, for instance, John 5:19, 24, 25; 6:26, 32, 47, 53; 8:34, 51, 58.

In a time of senselessness and ignorance (vv. 21-22), Asaph questioned this very thing. Seeing the prosperity of the wicked led to Asaph's crisis of faith. His feet almost slipped. He came close to stumbling (v. 2). Seeing the ease and wealth of those who opposed God made Asaph doubt whether God was good to His people. Asaph doubted whether keeping a pure heart was of any benefit before the Lord. He would later come to see those doubts as the musings of a man senseless and ignorant. The thinking of one who doubts God's goodness is likened to that of a beast (v. 22) - temporal, simple, and ignorant.

Scripture affirms repeatedly that God is good.[2] The word used by Asaph here is טוֹב (tob), meaning, "good, generous, festive, beautiful, or pleasing."[3] It most commonly carries the idea of a benevolence[4] which acts for the benefit of others.

We see it illustrated in a multitude of ways in Scripture, in Creation, and most certainly in the redemption of sinners. God's goodness is something that can be observed and experienced by His creatures.

---

2. Some philosophers have raised the question as to the nature of the standard of goodness. Is "goodness" a standard outside of God to which God conforms, or is God Himself the standard of what is to be regarded as "good"? This is referred to as the Euthyphro Problem, deriving its name from Plato's question in Euthyphro, namely, "Is piety what the gods say it is, or do the gods command piety because of its intrinsic nature apart from their own wishes?" It is observed that if God is the standard of goodness, then goodness is subject to the arbitrary whims of a personal deity. In other words, God could call something "good" today that tomorrow He calls "evil." Conversely, if goodness is some standard outside of God, something independent of Him, then He is subordinate to an abstract concept of goodness. If this is perplexing to you, I would recommend John Frame's treatment of this subject in his excellent book, *The Doctrine of God*, specifically pages 405-409.

3. J. Swanson, *Dictionary of Biblical Languages with Semantic Domains : Hebrew (Old Testament)* (electronic ed.). Oak Harbor: Logos Research Systems, Inc., 1997.

4. John M. Frame, *A Theology of Lordship*, vol. 2, *The Doctrine of God* (Phillipsburg: P & R Publishing, 2002), 410.

Psalm 34:8–10:

8 O taste and see that the Lord is good;

How blessed is the man who takes refuge in Him!

9 O fear the Lord, you His saints;

For to those who fear Him there is no want.

10 The young lions do lack and suffer hunger;

But they who seek the Lord shall not be in want of any good thing.

Psalm 84:11:

11 For the Lord God is a sun and shield;

The Lord gives grace and glory;

No good thing does He withhold from those who walk uprightly.

Often in Scripture, God's goodness is linked to some of His other attributes, such as His lovingkindness, His faithfulness, and His grace or mercy.

Psalm 86:5:

5 For You, Lord, are good, and ready to forgive,

And abundant in lovingkindness to all who call upon You.

Psalm 100:5:

5 For the Lord is good;

His lovingkindness is everlasting

And His faithfulness to all generations.

Psalm 106:1:

1 Praise the Lord!

Oh give thanks to the Lord, for He is good;

For His lovingkindness is everlasting.

Psalm 107:1:
1 Oh give thanks to the Lord, for He is good,
    For His lovingkindness is everlasting.

Psalm 118:1:
1 Give thanks to the Lord, for He is good;
    For His lovingkindness is everlasting.

Psalm 136:1:
1 Give thanks to the Lord, for He is good,
    For His lovingkindness is everlasting.

The goodness of God is the impetus for our praise, worship, and thanksgiving. He is worthy of these things because He is good. Since God is good, He is the source of all good things. Because His nature is good, all His deeds are done in righteousness and they are good. Every good thing finds its origin in Him. James 1:17: "Every good thing given and every perfect gift is from above, coming down from the Father of lights, with whom there is no variation or shifting shadow."

Psalm 85:12:
12 Indeed, the Lord will give what is good,
    And our land will yield its produce."

Psalm 103:5:
5 Who satisfies your years with good things,
    So that your youth is renewed like the eagle.

The Pure in Heart

Specifically, Asaph has in mind God's particular goodness to Israel. Though God was certainly good to His elect nation, even when that nation was populated mostly by rebellious and unbelieving Jews, the goodness described here is enjoyed by

21

those "who are pure in heart." The two phrases of verse 1 are parallel phrases that describe each other.

The expressions of goodness that are the focus of Psalm 73 were not enjoyed by all Israelites, but specifically those Jews who were uniquely God's people through regeneration. Though every Jew might enjoy the benefits of being part of the covenant nation, not every Jew was righteous and redeemed. This is what Paul was referring to in Romans 9:6-7 when he wrote, "For they are not all Israel who are descended from Israel; nor are they all children because they are Abraham's descendants." Being a Jew did not guarantee one's salvation.

The "pure in heart" are those who were redeemed, whom God had chosen, regenerated, and drawn near to Himself (Psalm 65:4). They were the righteous, those justified by God. They had believed His promise and were in right standing before Him through His redeeming grace.

By contrast, the wicked that Asaph speaks of in this psalm would include, but not be limited to, unredeemed, rebellious, unbelieving Jews. Asaph most certainly could be speaking of Gentile unbelievers, for there were plenty of examples of gentile God-haters prospering in their wickedness. But what transpired in a distant nation hundreds of miles away would not likely cause the vexation that Asaph experienced. The ease of life and prosperity that was before Asaph's eyes (v. 3) was most likely that enjoyed by his fellow Jews who gave no thought to purifying their life or pursuing obedience to God's commands.

These men are described as "arrogant," "wicked" (v. 3), "prideful," and "violent" (v. 4). They are mockers who "wickedly speak," setting "their mouth against the heavens" (v. 9). That they do not enjoy the blessing of salvation is evident from the fact that Asaph says they will be cast down to destruction (v. 18) and perish (v. 27). The ones who are destroyed in the next life are the very same ones who enjoy prosperity and ease in this life.

When Asaph says God is good to those who are pure in heart, he has in mind specific expressions of God's goodness enjoyed only by those who are pure in heart. These are described later in the psalm. Those who are pure in heart enjoy the continual presence of God (v. 23), the guidance and counsel of God, and the promise of eternal glory (v. 24). For the pure in heart, God is a greater treasure than anything else on earth (v. 25) because God is the strength and portion of a believer forever (v. 26). The good enjoyed by the righteous is the nearness of God Who is their refuge.

The answer for Asaph's struggle over the prosperity of the wicked was not to deny that the wicked enjoy good things, but to understand that those good things are only temporary and illusory. The good enjoyed by the righteous is an eternal good. It is a greater good by far. *I think that all things are good that God does - "prosperity" is a human perspective - All*

Psalm 73 and "Common Grace"

"Common Grace" is a term that some use to describe the good things enjoyed by impenitent sinners. The impenitent wicked enjoy many of the same pleasures, delights, and joys that come to God's people. Unbelievers get to taste good food, see beautiful sunsets, enjoy the delights of marriage, family, and recreation just as the righteous do. Further, unbelievers can find satisfaction in their work, enjoy the fruit of their labors, and delight in their material gains. The rain falls on the just and the unjust. This is what we typically call common grace.

Some reformed theologians also categorize God's restraint of sinful humanity and man's positive accomplishments in history as

23

God's gift to fallen men and thus expressions of common grace.[5] In short, common grace refers to graces from God that are commonly enjoyed by all men, the elect and the non-elect alike.

There are some reformed theologians who deny that God gives any blessings at all to those who are not His people.[6] They contend that it is inconceivable that God should be in any way, at any time, graciously inclined to those who are not His elect people. Further, they believe that Psalm 73 explicitly teaches that truth.

In his book titled *Prosperous Wicked and Plagued Saints: An Exposition of Psalm 73*, David J. Engelsma contends:

> Only to Israel is God good. This is incontrovertibly the teaching of verse 1: To Israel is God good, and to none else. That the teaching of verse 1 is the exclusive goodness of God to Israel becomes immediately plain as

---

5. A helpful series of articles by Cornelius Van Til appeared in the *Westminster Theological Journal*. I was unable to determine when the articles were first published. They are based on a paper that was read to The Calvinistic Philosophy Club at its Autumn 1941 meeting in Philadelphia. The links provided here are to that three-part series of articles.
http://files1.wts.edu/uploads/images/files/WTJ/CVT%20-%20Common%20Grace,%20pt%201.pdf
http://files1.wts.edu/uploads/images/files/WTJ/CVT%20-%20Common%20Grace,%20pt%202.pdf
http://files1.wts.edu/uploads/images/files/WTJ/CVT%20-%20Common%20Grace,%20pt%203.pdf
6. Within the reformed camp, there are theologians on both sides of this issue. One can be a "Calvinist" and affirm the reformation doctrines of Sovereign Grace without denying the doctrine of common grace. John Calvin affirmed that God gives a number of blessings and graces to those who are not His people, arguing that such "graces," though not salvific in nature or intent, are nonetheless expressions of a gracious God toward those who are impenitently under His wrath. Abraham Kuyper defended the doctrine of common grace, seeing no inherent contradiction between his own Calvinistic Theology and a belief in God's gracious treatment of unbelievers. See Van Til's articles mentioned in footnote 5.

God is ALWAYS good - all 24 of His actions are always good eternally.

soon as one tries to read the verse differently: "Truly good to Israel is God, and also to the wicked."[7]

Engelsma believes that Asaph's positive affirmation of God's goodness to His people necessarily denies that God is good to anyone else. Further, he writes, "Besides, the argument of the psalm in the verses that follow contends that, although it seems God is good to the wicked, in fact He is not good to them - not at all."[8]

why?

Engelsma boldly declares:

Psalm 73 refutes the lie of common grace. It demolishes this theory. **It is the purpose of the Holy Spirit with this psalm to deny the doctrine of common grace.** The psalm exposes the error of common grace plainly and directly. The psalm does not deny that God gives many good earthly gifts to the ungodly, so that, as a rule, their lives are comfortable, pleasurable, and successful. On the contrary, the psalm affirms that this is the case. This is the problem for the God-fearing psalmist. But the psalm denies that these gifts and these circumstances are God's blessing. By these material gifts and in these earthly circumstances, God is not good to the ungodly.[9] *NOT GOOD?*

I believe it would be fair to Engelsma's position to say that he believes all the "good" things enjoyed by unbelievers are not, in fact, intended by God for their welfare, but only for their ultimate destruction. He does not deny that the wicked enjoy ease of life and material prosperity, but with "these circumstances and

---

7. Engelsma, Kindle Locations 144-147.
8. Ibid., Kindle Locations 149-150.
9. Ibid., Kindle Locations 176-181. Emphasis mine.

possessions, God neither intends nor accomplishes their welfare."[10]

It is beyond the scope of this chapter to offer a fully-formed defense of the doctrine of common grace; I would refer you to the writings of Calvin, Kuyper, and Berkhof. For our purposes here, we need to consider whether Psalm 73 itself "destroys the notion of common grace," as Engelsma contends. Does Asaph's statement, "God is good to Israel," necessarily mean that God is good to Israel[11] alone?

It is reading into the text to assert that God is good to none but His own since the text does not say that. In verse 1, Asaph is affirming what he had started to doubt, namely whether God was truly good to His own. He doubted whether there was any benefit to a righteous life given the prosperity of the unrighteous (vv. 13-14) which was before him. From the vantage point of a changed perspective (vv. 16-17) Asaph affirmed that God is indeed good to the pure in heart. Asaph nowhere denies God is good to the wicked, he only affirms that God is good to the righteous.

The psalm has in mind a particular goodness that God shows to the righteous. The goodness shown to Israel in verse 1 is described in the last half of the psalm. These include guidance from God, the nearness of God, and eternal glory (vv. 21-28). These expressions of goodness are not shown to the wicked. These good things are enjoyed only by God's people, the elect, those whom He chooses and draws near to Himself. These good things are salvific in nature, covenant blessings that come to His

---

10. Ibid., Kindle Location 168.
11 .Engelsma also equates the Church and Israel, saying, "Israel is the church." Thus he contends that there is no distinction between what we would call Israel and what we would call the Church. This is a presupposition with which I would not concur. (Kindle Location 141)

own through the cross of Christ. These "goods" are the "goodest goods" which the wicked do not enjoy.

When Asaph says, "God is good to those who are pure in heart," he is speaking of riches enjoyed by only the righteous redeemed. To say that the impenitent, unrighteous wicked do not enjoy salvific blessings is not to say that they do not enjoy any blessings. It is one thing to say the wicked do not enjoy the grace of salvation; it is another to suggest that they don't receive any grace at all. We can affirm that God's ultimate good is reserved for His people without denying that God does any good to those who are not His people.

It is proper to say that Psalm 73 denies that God gives covenant blessings to the wicked. Psalm 73 does affirm that God gives these only to those "who are pure in heart." These are not "common graces" but "special graces." Those who affirm that God gives some common graces to all men (as I would) do not believe that salvation, election, and eternal glory are among them.

That God is kind, gracious, and good to all of His creatures (including the wicked reprobate) is clearly set forth in a number of places.

Psalm 145:8-9:
8 The Lord is gracious and merciful;
　　Slow to anger and great in lovingkindness.
9 The Lord is good to all,
　　And His mercies are over all His works.

In Psalm 145, David affirms that God is good to *all* and His mercies are over *all His works*. These mercies include His slowness to anger and His lovingkindness. God is gracious. Are "all His works" limited to Israel and Israel alone? Is not every heartbeat enjoyed by the wicked as a stay from immediate judgment due to the gracious, long-suffering mercy of God? How then can anyone contend that God is not gracious and kind to the wicked? Though I would never suggest that such grace and kindness will continue indefinitely, we cannot deny that it is being shown now.

Psalm 145 has more to say on this.

Psalm 145:13–16:
13 Your kingdom is an everlasting kingdom,
    And Your dominion endures throughout all generations.
14 The Lord sustains all who fall
    And raises up all who are bowed down.
15 The eyes of all look to You,
    And You give them their food in due time.
16 You open Your hand
    And satisfy the desire of every living thing.

Every living thing, or only the elect? Every living thing or only Israel? The fact that the wicked do not starve to death or are not deprived of oxygen and water for their sins is due to God's graciousness and kindness. It is a stretch to suggest that God gives no good thing, no blessing, and shows no kindness at all to unbelievers in this life. If an unbeliever and I sit down at the same table in the same restaurant and enjoy a steak dinner together, how is it that my steak is a gift from God but his is not?

Jesus commands us to love our enemies, modeling the gracious, loving character of our Heavenly Father who "causes His sun to rise on the evil and the good, and sends rain on the righteous and the unrighteous" (Matthew 5:45). We are to show kindness and love to our enemies because the Father does the same.

Paul said to unbelievers in Acts 14:17 that God "did not leave Himself without witness, in that He did good and gave [them] rains from heaven and fruitful seasons, satisfying [their] hearts with food and gladness." God gave unbelievers rains. God satisfied their hearts with food and gladness. These are evidences of God's good nature, a nature He displays to all His works through His kind provision and, yes, common grace.

There are examples in Scripture of God blessing unbelievers and their households. In Genesis 39, we read that God blessed the household of Potiphar because of Joseph. Genesis 39:5: "It came about that from the time he made him overseer in his house and over all that he owned, the Lord blessed the Egyptian's house on account of Joseph; thus the Lord's blessing was upon all that he owned, in the house and in the field." Potiphar was an unbeliever with an unbelieving wife, yet the Lord blessed him. It is true that the Lord blessed Potiphar because of Joseph, but He was blessed by God nonetheless.

Matthew Henry rightly noted, "Though wicked people receive many of the gifts of His providential bounty, yet we must own that He is, in a peculiar manner, good to Israel; they have favours from Him which others have not."[12]

I would respectfully disagree with the assertion that Psalm 73 destroys the doctrine of common grace. Psalm 73 does teach the doctrine of special grace toward "Israel" and "those who are pure in heart," but it does nothing to undermine the doctrine of common grace.

The Goodness of God and Eternal Damnation

God is good to Israel, to those who are pure in heart. God is good to His creation, and God is good to all men because God is good. Goodness is an essential quality of God's nature and being. God is good and can only do what is good. If it were possible for

---

12. Matthew Henry, *Matthew Henry's Commentary on the Whole Bible: Complete and Unabridged in One Volume* (Peabody: Hendrickson, 1994), 847.

God to do something that is not good, then we could not say that God is wholly good. God can only do what is good because God is only good.

Some people have a hard time squaring the "goodness of God" with the truth of "eternal ~~damnation.~~ *justice.*" If God is good, how can He send people to Hell to suffer eternally for their sins? Many people assume that God's goodness overrides His justice and ensures that all will be saved in the end.[13]

Many unbelievers, who are quick to proclaim their own goodness, trust in God's goodness to keep them out of Hell. "Surely," they reason, "God is good and would never send me to Hell." Yet, ironically, the very thing they are trusting in to save them - namely, the goodness of God - is that which will damn them everlastingly.

Because God is good, He must see that justice is done. Imagine your loved one, spouse, parent, or child was brutally beaten and murdered by a violent criminal. Eventually the perpetrator was found, arrested, and charged with the crime. During his trial, all the evidence of his guilt was methodically presented by the prosecution. There were eye-witnesses, DNA evidence at the scene, an established motive, and the crime was even caught on videotape. Not only that, mounds of circumstantial evidence was presented, establishing the criminal's guilt beyond all reasonable doubt.

Then imagine that the day of sentencing arrives and you watch as the judge, charged with seeing that justice is done, makes the following startling announcement:

"Ladies and Gentlemen of the Jury, family and friends of the victim present, I wish to inform you that the guilt of the accused has been conclusively established beyond all reasonable doubt.

---

13. Rob Bell takes the same logic applied to the love of God to argue for a form of universalism in his book *Love Wins*.

However, since I am a *good* judge, and since I am a *good* person, I wish to display my *goodness* by letting the accused go free. All charges are henceforth dismissed." *hello Scott - "I chose grace"*

Then you watch as the guilty criminal walks down the aisle and past you to freedom without paying for his violent crime against your loved one. Do you stand up at that point and applaud the judge for his display of goodness? Do you exit the courtroom commenting to your friends and family, "Wow, that was sure a good judge!"?

Does that repudiation of justice cause you to admire the judge's goodness? Or do you think that a "good" judge must see that justice is done? Certainly we can say that although the guilty criminal may think the judge has been good to him, the surviving family does not feel that the judge has been good to them, or the victim, or society at large.

God is good, and because God is good, He must see that justice is done. All sin will be paid for. It will either be paid for by the atoning death of Christ on the cross, or by the impenitent sinner in eternal conscious torment. The goodness of God does not undermine the doctrine of eternal Hell; the goodness of God demands an eternal Hell.[14]

Just as a good earthly judge does not pervert justice, turn a blind eye to crimes, or release guilty criminals, so the eternal Heavenly Judge will not do so either. God will not wink at sin. He will not pervert the eternal demands of His holy justice. He will not turn a blind eye to rape, murder, lying, blasphemy, and theft. Every impenitent sinner who dies without repenting and trusting

---

14. The fact that Hell is eternal is also seen as incompatible with the goodness of God. However, those who object to Hell being a place of eternal conscious torment do not grasp the sinfulness of sin and how much any and every sin is an affront to a Holy God. For a defense of the doctrine of eternal Hell, see *Sinners in the Hands of a Good God: Reconciling Divine Judgment and Mercy* by David Clotfelter.

Thank you Lord for protecting my mind - Keeping

Christ will have his or her day in court. Since God is good, justice will be served. *cant humanistic bad doctrine -*

Unbelievers think the goodness of God is their hope. It will be their undoing. For the believer, the goodness of God is their assurance that, as those chosen and loved by God, they will experience eternal good. Because God is good, He will not punish or cast off those who have trusted in His Son (John 6:35-44).

Though some may affirm that justice is good, they may say that it is not good for those who receive it. This raises the objection in another form: if God does something not-good to the unbeliever, then God is not completely good. The assumption behind the objection is that since God is good, He is obligated to do good to all of His creatures all of the time.

In his book *The Doctrine of God*, John Frame offers some helpful considerations.[15]

First, in the damnation of sinners, God does not do something that is "not-good" or "bad." In fact, the damnation of sinners is demanded by His justice. It is, as already noted, an expression of His goodness. If the eternal damnation of sinners were unjust, unrighteous, or capricious, then it would not be good. That would indicate that God is not good. Punishing the wicked for their sins is not a bad thing.

If God only does good to those who are not condemned to Hell, it does not mean that He has done something bad to the others. For God to withhold good from some creature is not in itself a bad thing, nor does it impugn His character. God is not obligated to do a positive good toward creatures that are undeserving of that goodness. If God withholds good and gives justice instead, He has done no wrong.

---

15. I am indebted to John Frame's observations in his book *The Doctrine of God* (P&R Publishing), pages 412-414.

us safely, close to you. I pray that you will guard my family from error. Keep them away from schemes and traps that ensnare the mind, develop

God doctrine and produce death.

Second, the punishment of sinners accomplishes a great good, namely, the display of God's justice and righteousness. Any time that God's attributes are manifested, displayed, or proclaimed, it is good. For eternity, the wrath of God against sinners and rebels will be poured out as a demonstration of His justice, His righteousness and the vindication of His Word and law. That is a GREAT good!

Third, the damnation of the impenitent wicked is a good done to and for God's people. It is a great act of benevolence by God toward His people that He would triumph over their enemies, vindicate His good name, and punish those who have caused His people so much suffering. As Paul says in 2 Thessalonians 1:5–10:

> This is a plain indication of God's righteous judgment so that you will be considered worthy of the kingdom of God, for which indeed you are suffering. For after all it is only just for God to repay with affliction those who afflict you, and to give relief to you who are afflicted and to us as well when the Lord Jesus will be revealed from Heaven with His mighty angels in flaming fire, dealing out retribution to those who do not know God and to those who do not obey the gospel of our Lord Jesus. These will pay the penalty of eternal destruction, away from the presence of the Lord and from the glory of His power, when He comes to be glorified in His saints on that day, and to be marveled at among all who have believed - for our testimony to you was believed.

When God establishes His justice, He is doing good to His people. It is for the sake of His people that God banishes rebels from His Heaven and eventually the New Earth. Therefore, in punishing the wicked, God is being good to His people.

Fourth, it might be that in some sense, God's punishment of the wicked in Hell is, in fact, an expression of His goodness toward them. As Frame writes:

> It may also be worth considering that in their very punishment in Hell, God is giving a privilege to the lost - the privilege of displaying His justice and His victory in the spiritual war (cf. Rom. 9:17). Those who find no benevolence in this privilege might be advised to consider whether their standards of goodness are sufficiently theocentric.[16]

In other words, it may, in fact, be that God is doing good to the lost in allowing them to display the glory of His justice against sin. Admittedly, that is a hard pill to swallow, but if we think that is abhorrent, we should ask ourselves if perhaps we might have an inadequate understanding of what is truly "good."

Fifth, it must be recognized that their punishment in Hell notwithstanding, God has shown plenty of goodness to the lost. Again, Frame writes:

> A somewhat more satisfying answer to the question is that God is good to creatures in different ways and at different times, depending on their natures and their roles in God's plan for history. His goodness does not obligate Him to give the same blessings to all, or to give the same blessings to any creature throughout his existence. If the lost in Hell are now receiving no blessings at all, they cannot complain that God was never good to them. During this life, they were surrounded by God's goodness, just like all other creatures. Furthermore, as Scripture often represents it, the wicked

---

16. Frame, 413.

typically prosper in this life and oppress the righteous. In the next life, these roles are reversed (Luke 16:19-31). So even the reprobate should confess that God has been good to them, far more than they deserved.[17]

The wicked in Hell cannot deny that they have had a rich experience of God's goodness on this earth, which goodness they turned to their own condemnation by their rebellion and rejection of truth.

In summary, the doctrine of God's goodness is not incompatible with the doctrine of eternal punishment.

Psalm 73:2
But as for me, my feet came close to stumbling,
My steps had almost slipped.

Here we are introduced to Asaph's struggle. He confessed that God is good to His people. That was the great truth Asaph learned through his struggle. This confidence in the goodness of God had not always been the disposition of his heart. He nearly fell from this confidence. He nearly wavered from this conviction.

This is the account of Asaph's personal struggle of faith, his near apostasy. Asaph is not writing about another. He is not describing the experience of someone he knew. The truths of this psalm are not the theorizing of an ivory tower intellectual, but a real struggle by a real man of God. His struggle is shared with us so that we might receive the benefit of His understanding without suffering the pain of his doubts.

Asaph observed the same thing the righteous in every generation observe: the apparent prosperity of the wicked (v. 3). Asaph almost concluded it was vain for him to keep his heart pure

---

17. Ibid.

and live a righteous life (v. 13). He wondered if he would be better off living like the wicked. His faith was nearly shaken. Asaph's envy of the wicked had robbed him of his joy (v. 21) and nearly made shipwreck of his faith.

His feet had almost slipped. The word translated "slipped" means, "to pour out."[18] It is the image of water being poured out so that it spreads around, going beyond its boundaries, and leaving the place and path appointed for it. Like water spilled outside a container, Asaph found himself thinking in ways outside of God's truth. When the clear constraints of God's revealed truth are doubted and cast aside, our feet will wander anywhere and everywhere, taking us into apostasy. Just as right thinking drives right living, so wrong thinking results in wrong living.

When our feet stand on God's truth, we are safe. When we wander from that path, we are immediately in dangerous territory. In short order, when not guided by truth in the bounds of revelation, we run into error, apostasy and spiritual shipwreck. Asaph nearly stumbled over the apparent prosperity of the wicked. This would have brought spiritual ruin to his life and the lives of countless others.

This is a real spiritual danger to God's people. Without an eternal perspective on the wicked and their seeming prosperity, the righteous, even the most godly, can be easily deceived. They begin to doubt the goodness of God and start to question whether there is any benefit to serving the Almighty. This dangerous temptation, this thief of Christian joy and contentment, is best answered by a right perspective on wealth and eternity.

---

18. R. L. Thomas, *New American Standard Hebrew-Aramaic and Greek Dictionaries: Updated Edition* (electronic ed.). Anaheim: Foundation Publications, Inc.

Therein lies the great value of this psalm. It is an aid to your spiritual preservation.

The Lessons We Learn

There are three great truths we can take away from these first two verses:

First, the righteous can indeed struggle with this seeming inequity. From all indicators, Asaph was a godly Jew, greatly gifted by God and used in service to His people in their worship. Asaph was a man with a deep and rich understanding of the Old Testament Scriptures. That is evident from the psalms he wrote (Psalms 50, 73-83). It is possible for even godly and mature believers to lose perspective and be severely tempted and tried. Matthew Henry writes, "The faith even of strong believers may sometimes be sorely shaken and ready to fail them. There are storms that will try the firmest anchors."[19] If you have ever found yourself in that spiritual swamp, you are not alone - but that does not mean you should stay there! Psalm 73 warns us of a real spiritual danger we should not take lightly.

Second, God, in and by His grace, keeps His own from falling. Asaph's feet almost slipped. He came close to stumbling. Almost-slipping is not slipping. Close-to-stumbling is not stumbling. Though God's people may feel as if their faith is about to break and fail them, it will not. Though the righteous may feel they are on the brink of spiritual apostasy, God does not allow His people to fall away and finally perish.

> Those that shall never be quite undone are sometimes very near it, and, in their own apprehension, as good as gone. Many a precious soul, that shall live forever, had once a very narrow turn for its life; almost and well-nigh

---

19. Henry, 847.

ruined, but a step between it and fatal apostasy, and yet snatched as a brand out of the burning, which will forever magnify the riches of divine grace in the nations of those that are saved.[20]

John Hooper, writing in the early 1500s, said:

There is to be noted that the prophet said he was almost gone, and not altogether. Here is the presence, providence, strength, safeguard, and keeping of man by Almighty God, marvelously set forth. That although we are tempted and brought even to the very point to perpetrate and do all mischief, yet he stays us and keeps us, that the temptation shall not overcome us.[21]

Asaph owed his preservation from spiritual shipwreck not to his own reason, his own brilliance, or his own spiritual strength, but to the keeping power of God. God gave him a proper perspective. God opened his eyes to see the true condition of the wicked, and the true end of their wealth. Asaph was preserved in his faith by God's keeping grace. Asaph was preserved from stumbling and slipping because He belonged to God. Such is the safe and secure position owned by each and every true believer.

Third, the truth of God's goodness toward His own is the sure foundation upon which the righteous may trust. Where Asaph begins, we must begin - with the firm conviction that God is good to those who are pure in heart.

With this truth as our anchor and starting point, we have a north star by which we can navigate the tempestuous waters of life's inequities. All the circumstances and deceptions of this life, all that we evaluate with our own human understanding, can cast

---

20. Ibid., pp. 847–848.
21. Charles Haddon Spurgeon, *The Treasury of David,* Vol. 2, *Psalms 58-110* (Peabody: Hendrickson Publishers), 257.

us upon the rocks of doubt and trouble. We must always come back to our firm conviction that God is good to those who are His. He is eternally good.

This truth cannot be shaken. We must resolve to carve this truth deep into our hearts, to live by this truth and die by this truth. The Christian may not be able to reconcile all of God's providential workings with that truth, but we believe it nonetheless. We may not at times see how those things that God allows into our life are expressions of His goodness. We may not in the moment understand how God's goodness can square with the apparent prosperity of the wicked and the affliction of the righteous, but we must never doubt that it does.

We should always return to this anchor for the soul: God is good to those who are pure in heart. Henry remarks, "These are truths which cannot be shaken and which we must resolve to live and die by. Though we may not be able to reconcile all the disposals of Providence with them, we must believe they are reconcilable."[22]

Such confidence will serve as the means by which God preserves us in trouble and times of intense temptation.

As Charles Spurgeon wrote:

It is well to make sure of what we do know, for this will be good anchor-hold for us when we are molested by those mysterious storms which arise from things which we do not understand. Whatever may or may not be the truth about mysterious and inscrutable things, there are certainties somewhere; experience has placed some tangible facts within our grasp; let us, then, cling to these, and they will prevent our being carried away by those hurricanes of infidelity which still come from the

---

22. Henry, 847.

wilderness, and, like whirlwinds, smite the four corners of our house and threaten to overthrow it. O my God, however perplexed I may be, let me never think ill of Thee. If I cannot understand Thee, let me never cease to believe in Thee. It must be so, it cannot be otherwise, Thou art good to those whom Thou hast made good; and where Thou hast renewed the heart Thou wilt not leave it to its enemies.[23]

Surely God is good to those who are pure in heart!

---

23. Spurgeon, 246.

2

A Treasure Admired

Psalm 73:3
For I was envious of the arrogant
As I saw the prosperity of the wicked.

Looks can be deceiving.

The Scriptures repeatedly warn us of the folly of judging by outward appearances.

Saul may have stood head and shoulders above the rest of his countrymen (1 Samuel 10:23) and been more handsome than all of them (1 Samuel 9:2), but those features do not a faithful king make. Samuel would never have thought that David would be God's choice to replace Saul. He thought David's brother Eliab was the Lord's anointed, chosen to replace Saul, but the Lord said to Samuel, "Do not look at his appearance or at the height of his stature, because I have rejected him; for God sees not as man sees, for man looks at the outward appearance, but the Lord looks at the heart" (1 Samuel 16:7). Though David's son, Absalom, was strikingly handsome, he was a wicked young man who rebelled against the throne, defiled His father's concubines, and sought to kill David (2 Samuel 14:25; 15:1-17:29).

False teachers hide their true identity by donning sheep's clothing (Matthew 7:15). Satan deceives by appearing as an angel of light (2 Corinthians 11:14). Tares grow among the wheat and appear as genuine believers (Matthew 13:25-40). False converts adopt the language, culture, and conventions of their Christian counterparts. They are able to fool everyone around them and their true nature is only revealed when they finally apostatize (1 John 2:19).

Life is full of examples of the deceptive power of appearances. You know that the email you received from a Saudi Prince wanting to give you 10% of his family's $30 million fortune for the simple kindness of sending him $1,000 to facilitate the money transfer is a fraud. Companies spend millions to convince us that their product is bigger, brighter, and better than any other. Politics is the art of making us think that someone who does not share our values, deeply cares about our values. We are not wooed by the candidate but by how we perceive the candidate. The grass is always greener on the other side of the fence. Unfortunately, it is not until we jump the fence that we find out the grass was planted over a septic tank.

We are not just deceived by appearances, we are *easily* deceived by appearances.

The wicked appear to be blessed. In Psalm 73, it looked to Asaph as if their wickedness was ignored by God. From all appearances, the wicked enjoyed an easy life and the favor of God. At least that is how it seemed. Asaph was drawn away and led astray by what he saw.

Looks can be deceiving.

Soul-Poisoning Envy

In the previous chapter, we examined Asaph's confession of early stumbling by doubting God's goodness. His feet nearly slipped from the path of righteousness.

In verses 3-5, Asaph described the comforts and material blessings enjoyed by the wicked. In verses 6-12 he described their pride, their wickedness, and their hostility to God. The prosperity of the wicked made Asaph conclude that it was vain to "keep his heart pure" and "wash his hands in innocence."

Seeing the prosperity described in verses 3-5 gave birth to the sin of envy in Asaph's heart. He candidly confessed, "I was envious of the arrogant as I saw the prosperity of the wicked."

The word translated "envious" is sometimes translated "jealousy." According to the *Theological Wordbook of the Old Testament*:

> This verb expresses a very strong emotion whereby some quality or possession of the object is desired by the subject. This root occurs eighty-seven times....The term may be used in a purely descriptive sense to denote one of the characteristics of living men (Ecclesiastes 9:6), or in a derogatory sense to denote hostile and disruptive passions (Proverbs 27:4), or in a favorable sense to denote consuming zeal focused on one that is loved (Psalm 69:9 [H 10]).[1]

Envy took root in the heart of Asaph. He had a "strong emotion," a hostile and disruptive passion to possess the prosperity of the wicked. The specific things that Asaph envied are described later in the passage.

---

1. R. L. Harris, G. L. Archer Jr., & B. K. Waltke (Eds.), *Theological Wordbook of the Old Testament* (electronic ed., p. 802). Chicago: Moody Press.

Envy is sin. It is the strong emotion of jealousy over the advantage or blessings enjoyed by another. This is not an innocent desire or a simple want of something; rather, envy desires what another has. Envy longs for the blessing or favor that another enjoys. Envy is a dangerous, soul-destroying sin.

Edom was envious of the favor God gave to Israel. That envy was accompanied by hatred and anger (Ezekiel 35:11, 15). The nation of Edom even rejoiced over the downfall and desolation of Israel when they fell under God's judgment (Obadiah 10-14), going so far as to help Israel's enemies ransack the nation. Envy is the sin that made Joseph's brothers resent him and eventually plot his murder (Genesis 37:11). Though they did not end up murdering Joseph, in their envy they did sell him into slavery. In their envy, they lied to their father Jacob for over twenty years about the fate of their brother.

The sin of envy led the religious leaders of Israel to hand Jesus over to Pilate to be crucified (Matthew 27:18). It appears on the list of the deeds of the flesh (Galatians 5:21) and is among those things that characterize unbelievers who do not acknowledge God and have been "given over to a depraved mind, to do those things which are not proper" (Romans 1:28-29). Paul says in Titus 3:3 that the sin of envy once characterized every one of us: "For we also once were foolish ourselves, disobedient, deceived, enslaved to various lusts and pleasures, spending our life in malice and envy, hateful, hating one another." Sadly, it is also a sin which Christians can commit. We all know envy. We are well acquainted with it.

Envy is a fundamental discontent with what God in His good providence has provided. Envy is the lust for what we do not have. It is the opposite of contentment which is the godly disposition of spirit that is satisfied with what God has appointed.[2] Envy keeps us from enjoying the blessings we do possess, causing us to measure those rich blessings against richer blessings enjoyed by others. In that way, envy poisons the blessings God gives to us. Envy renders us unable to appreciate God's goodness because we are too busy resenting the goodness He shows to another. While sitting amidst a plethora of our own prosperity, envy causes us to only see the good things enjoyed by another. What should be causes of great rejoicing and thankfulness are turned to resentment and ingratitude. We become bitter over what we do not have instead of delighting in what we do. Truly, envy is evil.

The Christian who recognizes the sin of envy in his or her own heart needs to repent of that sin and turn to Christ for healing and forgiveness. We must pursue envy's opposite: contentment (Philippians 4:10-14). Pray that God will deliver you from envy and give you a hatred for this sin which robs you of the enjoyment of every other blessing!

Asaph looked upon the prosperity of the wicked and he wanted what they seemed to have. He envied the God-hater and desired the wealth and ease that they seemed to enjoy. It was envy that led Asaph to doubt the benefit of personal holiness. Envy led to an embittered heart (Psalm 73:21) that blinded Asaph to the riches of God's favor toward him (vv. 21-28). Ultimately Asaph doubted God's goodness, nearly stumbled to spiritual destruction, and came close to leading others astray (v. 15), all because of envy.

Truly envy is evil, but how much more so when it is those who are evil whom we envy?

---

2. For more on the subject of godly contentment I would recommend *The Rare Jewel of Christian Contentment* by Jeremiah Burroughs (The Banner of Truth Trust).

The Arrogant

Asaph describes those he envied as the "arrogant" and the "wicked." Notice the parallelism of the verse:

Psalm 73:3:
3 For I was envious of the arrogant
    As I saw the prosperity of the wicked.

Asaph is describing one group of people. These prosperous ones are described as both "arrogant" and "wicked."

The word translated as "arrogant" describes someone "in a state of improper pride and haughtiness."[3] That word has also been translated as "boastful." The KJV renders the word "foolish." Scripture often characterizes the foolish man as ignorant and prideful (Proverbs 14:16). The haughty, prideful, boastful demeanor of the wicked stands in stark contrast with the humble, gentle spirit enjoined upon the righteous.

Asaph described the pride of these wicked people later in the psalm when he wrote in verses 8-9:

8 They mock and wickedly speak of oppression;
    They speak from on high.
9 They have set their mouth against the heavens,
    And their tongue parades through the earth.

When Asaph described the objects of his envy as "arrogant" and "wicked" it served to highlight the folly of such envy. It would be bad enough to envy a wise man, a righteous man, or a humble man for some quality he displayed or some blessing he enjoyed.

---

3. J. Swanson, *Dictionary of Biblical Languages with Semantic Domains : Hebrew (Old Testament)* (electronic ed.). Oak Harbor: Logos Research Systems, Inc., 1997.

How foolish it is to envy an arrogant, wicked man! As Charles Spurgeon wisely noted, "... he must be a fool who envies fools." In connection with verse 3, Spurgeon also said, "It is a pitiful thing that an heir of Heaven should have to confess 'I was envious,' but worse still that he should have to put it, 'I was envious at the foolish.'"[4] Even Mr. T understood that it is better to "pity the fool" than to envy him.

It is not just Psalm 73 that warns us about envying arrogant, boastful, violent, and wicked men.

Proverbs 3:31:
31 Do not envy a man of violence
    And do not choose any of his ways.

Proverbs 23:17:
17 Do not let your heart envy sinners,
    But live in the fear of the LORD always.

Proverbs 24:1:
1 Do not be envious of evil men,
    Nor desire to be with them.

Proverbs 24:19-20:
19 Do not fret because of evildoers
    Or be envious of the wicked;
20 For there will be no future for the evil man;
    The lamp of the wicked will be put out.

David warned, "Do not fret because of evildoers, be not envious toward wrongdoers. For they will wither quickly like the grass and fade like the green herb" (Psalm 37:1–2).

---

4. Charles Haddon Spurgeon, *The Treasury of David*, Vol. 2, *Psalms 58-110* (Peabody: Hendrickson Publishers), 247.

Asaph looked upon their prosperity and he envied them, but when he looked upon their ultimate perishing, he realized there was truly nothing to envy (Psalm 73:27). When a righteous man envies the wicked fool, he is in desperate need of reorientation!

Their Prosperity

The riches of this world can be quite alluring. We live in a world that revolves around the power of the almighty dollar. We are told in every advertisement on TV or radio that money can buy happiness, contentment, and comfort. Slick Madison Avenue advertising firms seek to convince us our marriages would be happier if we spent more money at Kay Jewelers or your local Lexus dealership. They want us to believe our status in society is determined by the name brand of the shoes we wear, the car we drive, or the cell phone we use. If you listen to the advertisers, then you would believe that unlimited fawning from the opposite sex can be yours if you just use the right shampoo, razor, toothpaste, and body wash.

What do all of these things have in common? They cost money. All that stands between me and a new Lexus is money. All that stands between me and a happy marriage is money. Money makes the world go around. You have to have money to make money. Everybody wants money. Everybody needs money. Therefore, money is the answer to all of life's problems and perplexities.

Solomon perfectly summed up the perspective of a vain life under the sun in Ecclesiastes 10:19: "Men prepare a meal for enjoyment, and wine makes life merry, and money is the answer to everything." To that statement the entire world system shouts a hearty "Amen! Money is the answer to everything!"

Well, if money is the answer to everything, then those with more money have more answers to everything. Not only that, they have more everything! They enjoy more comforts, more ease, more conveniences, more pleasures, and more delights. We would expect that their problems would be fewer and their anxieties lighter. The age-old adage, "Money can't buy happiness," sounds like the wisdom of a fool uttered by someone who has never had money. It sure appears that those with money are happy. It certainly seems as if there is a direct correspondence between the amount of money and the amount of happiness.

Who among us has not secretly pined for the wealth of Bill Gates or Steve Jobs? Who hasn't given some thought to how much easier life would be with a couple million dollars in the bank? That would be enough to buy your freedom from the 9-to-5 grind at work. Have you ever sat down and made a mental list of all the anxieties, discomforts, and troubles that would instantly vanish if you won the Publishers Clearing House Sweepstakes? Haven't we all thought, for at least a moment, how much easier life would be if we were the winners of the last Powerball drawing?

Prosperity is alluring. Envy of the wealth and prosperity enjoyed by others is a temptation common to men - all too common.

Psalm 73:4
For there are no pains in their death,
And their body is fat.

In these two verses (vv. 3-4), Asaph described the blessings and comforts that he perceived were enjoyed by the wicked. In verse 3, he mentioned their prosperity. Here Asaph describes their ease of life and death.

It is worth noting that Asaph begins by describing the death of the wicked. The manner in which the wicked die was something that troubled him. We might expect him to describe the life of the wicked and then to talk about the manner in which they die. Asaph does not. I would suggest that Asaph began with the description of their death for two reasons.

First, the ease and comfort of their death perfectly portrays the ease and comfort of their lives. They died as they lived: untroubled and peaceful. The peacefulness of their death serves as a perfect capstone to a full life of abundant provision and increasing wealth. These are people who cannot lose! Not only does life fail to present them with difficulties, death treats them with kid gloves.

Second, it is in the death of the wicked that we might expect to see at least a partial reckoning for the great injustice of a life spent prospering in wickedness. Given that their lives have been attended by so much material ease and blessing, provision and comfort, we might hope there would at least be some comeuppance in their death. Yet it is not so. Thus, the manner in which the wicked die seems to be the highest evidence of their blessed state.

Hear Asaph's lament: **There are no pains in their death!** The unrighteous simply pass on. They step through the veil with ease. Their death is pain-free. They live in comfort and die in ease. They don't experience pain. They do not suffer from the long drawn-out agonies of illness and disease. They do not spend months in the deathbed slowly dying a miserable, painful, agonizing death.

Compare that with details of many godly and righteous people whose death has been accompanied with unspeakable pain. Like you, Asaph was familiar with pious believers who spent their final hours, weeks, or even months, in unrelenting and unmerciful agony. We know of godly believers whose final minutes in this life were accompanied by flames at the stake, lions in the arena, or pains at the hands of persecutors. We know of God-fearing men and women who have spent their final weeks wracked with cancer, pierced with infections, or riddled with chronic pain.

Should we not expect that in the final hours there would be some reckoning? Should we not expect to see a great reversal when it comes to the greatest enemy: death? We might hope to see that the righteous, in passing into eternity, might get a taste of the comfort and ease with which the unrighteous had lived their lives. Further, we might hope to see that the unrighteous might get a taste of the pain, discomfort, and agony suffered by many a righteous person.

Instead, the unrighteous glide off into eternity with hardly a care and nary a pain. There are no pains in their death. They are suddenly stricken by a heart attack or an aneurysm and die in a moment. They pass away painlessly in their sleep while enjoying the comfort of rest. These very wicked who have lived their lives opposing and oppressing the people of God drift away effortlessly into the afterlife. This appears to be a grievous injustice!

And their body is fat. This is a further lament concerning the condition in which they die. The King James Version translates that phrase, "But their strength is firm."[5] In other words, they are physically healthy, right to the very end.

Having lived the life of such abundant prosperity, they never went without. All of life's delicacies they enjoyed. While most people lived from hand to mouth, the wicked continually increased in wealth, living like kings and growing fat. Their death offered no reversal of fortune. They didn't seem to suffer any

---

5. *The Holy Bible: King James Version*. 2009 (Electronic Edition of the 1900 Authorized Version.) (Ps 73:4). Bellingham, WA: Logos Research Systems, Inc.

wasting disease over an extended time. Prior to their death, the unrighteous did not lose their strength, their muscle, their mobility, or their body mass. They died as plump as they lived. They seemed to leave this life as strong as they lived it.

Compare that picture with the many righteous people you know whose dying weeks and months sapped their bank accounts, drained them of energy, and left them as weak and frail shadows of their former selves. This seems like a tremendous injustice!

Another Kind of Pain

It is not just freedom from physical pain that the wicked enjoy, but it appears they are also free from any pains of conscience or emotion.

We might expect, when it comes down to the most solemn moment of their life - their death - that the unrighteous wicked might feel some twang of conscience or emotional agony. This does not seem to be the case. They have lived their lives in opposition to God. They have sinned against His law. They have violated their conscience, oppressed their fellow man, and given no thought to God for their entire lives. The wicked live their lives indulging the desires of their flesh without concern for God or His glory. Then they die without any pangs of conscience.

They do not spend their final hours in torment over their sin. They do not wrestle with their conscience, seeking to come to grips with the truth of eternal judgment. They pass into eternity without any regrets, appearing to die without a single care in the world. They are not terrified. They are not tormented. They are not worried. They die as they lived: mentally, emotionally, and spiritually at ease.

We tend to think of death as "the great equalizer." In one sense, that is true. All men die. As Solomon said in Ecclesiastes

3:20, "All go to the same place. All came from the dust and all return to the dust." All men, the righteous and the wicked, have to leave behind all that this earth provides and shuffle off this mortal coil. Naked we come into this world, and naked we shall leave (Job 1:21). Death strips us all of everything.

Though death is the great equalizer, all men don't die equally. From Asaph's perspective, the wicked die in comfort and ease. That is certainly different than what he observed regarding the death of the righteous. Many a righteous man has spent his final hours lamenting his sin and regretting a life not spent sufficiently for the glory of God. Many a pious believer passes into eternity still struggling with the enemy, wishing he had done more for his Lord, and lamenting his lack of sanctification. Far too many righteous men and women are tormented by doubts regarding their faith and salvation.

Job lamented the very same inequity. He compared his own suffering to the ease and prosperity of the wicked. Job's comforter, Zophar, claimed that "the triumphing of the wicked is short, and the joy of the godless momentary" (Job 20:5). Job sets the record straight by pointing out that the wicked do not suffer in their wickedness. Instead, they seem to prosper! Job says in Job 21:7-9, 13:

7 Why do the wicked still live,
　　Continue on, also become very powerful?
8 Their descendants are established with them in their sight,
　　And their offspring before their eyes,
9 Their houses are safe from fear,
　　And the rod of God is not on them.
13 They spend their days in prosperity,
　　And suddenly they go down to Sheol.

"Suddenly they go down to Sheol" expresses the same lament of Asaph in Psalm 73:4, namely, that the wicked live prosperous lives and die quick and easy deaths. Job observed that the wicked are quickly taken out of this life. They do not suffer the loss of all things as Job had. They do not end their lives as paupers or suffer a slow, agonizing death. Their lives are spent in prosperity, and their death is speedy.

We see plenty of examples of this very thing in our own day. We can relate to Asaph's observations. Saddam Hussein was executed quickly. He died by hanging. The leaked video of his execution showed him walking confidently to the gallows without fear while chanting the name of Allah. After only a few moments with a noose around his neck, he dropped quickly to his sudden death. He was plump. His body was fat. Yet, how many men, women, and children suffered and died, were starved and tormented and chased by pains all the way to their death at the hands of that wicked man? How many, who were far more righteous than he, wasted away to their death and died in pain and agony because of him? He prospered in his wickedness and died without pain. His body was fat.

Similarly, Osama bin Laden died from a bullet to the head while living in luxury, surrounded by his multiple wives who were there to meet his every need. It was quick. It was easy. How many people wasted away and died in excruciating pain because of him? He prospered in his wickedness.

Adolf Hitler died in the arms of his mistress. Compare his death to that of Dietrich Bonhoeffer, who died in prison, cold, hungry, and neglected. Their deaths were only days apart, but they could not be more different. How many, who were far more righteous than Hitler, suffered and died in agony under his hand and that of the Third Reich?

This just doesn't seem right, does it? You can see why these things were troublesome to Asaph (v. 16). Are you starting to feel the weight of this issue? Can you see why Asaph's heart became embittered and why he questioned God's goodness?

Psalm 73:5
They are not in trouble as other men,
Nor are they plagued like mankind.

It was not just the absence from pain and suffering in *death* of the wicked that Asaph noted, but their *life* seemed to be equally trouble-free.

It seems as if the wicked do not have to deal with the burdens of life that saddle the rest of us. Do the prosperous wicked have to fight the "battle for bread" like the righteous do? It doesn't seem that the prideful and irreligious are forced to work from sunup to sundown, slaving for the grain to bake a loaf of bread. They never have to worry where their next meal is coming from. They don't have to live from hand to mouth, from paycheck to paycheck. It sure doesn't seem that way.

Does Bill Gates ever wonder where his next meal is coming from? No. Did Steve Jobs ever lie awake at night worrying about his car breaking down? No. Do Al Gore or Nancy Pelosi have to deal with the landlord knocking on their door for the rent at the beginning of each and every month? Hardly. Each one of these people swims in wealth unimaginable to most of the folks reading this book. Yet they live their lives with no regard for God, His standards, or His Word. Further, they spend their money, which they seem to have in never-ending measure and abundance, to promote things that positively oppose the glory of God and His people.

The wicked live in a different world than we do. The things which consume our time, attention, and resources aren't even noticed by the prosperous wicked. We have to decide whether to buy new shoes for the kids or replace the hot-water heater this month. The righteous live their lives in fear that the car will need a repair, and that repair will put them behind on their doctor bills. These are the things that occupy mankind. These are the concerns that trouble us. The wicked seem as if they live in some special world where they are exempt from all these concerns. They're not in trouble like the rest of us.

The trials and troubles faced by the righteous every day seem to be without parallel in the lives of the rich, the famous, the prosperous wicked.

A Typical Day for You

You work all day long at a job you don't always enjoy, maybe never enjoy. After fighting all day long with coworkers, bosses, customers, and employees, you leave work relieved to have another eight hours in the bank and be done with another day.

When you stop to pick up the kids from school, you meet with the teacher and find out your child is not doing as well as he should in math. He needs to be tutored. Further, he got in a fight today at school, and spent some time in the principal's office. Oh, and he will need some money next week or he can't go on the field trip with the rest of the class. As you quietly drive home, you realize you should be spending more time with your children, helping them with their homework in order to get their grades up. After all, how can they hope to get into a decent college, get a job, or live a normal life, if they can't get a good education?

Your mind is taken off all the worries regarding your child's future by that squeaking and grinding noise coming from somewhere under your car as you turn the final corner for home.

You think to yourself, "I really should make an appointment with the mechanic to get that checked out." But where are you going to get the money for that?

As you pull into the yard, you realize that the lawn has to be mowed, and mowed tonight, since the forecast is predicting rain for the next week. How will you find time to mow the lawn? You have to make dinner first. Before you can make dinner, you have to clean up the kitchen, since it is still messy from last night. You would love to start cleaning, but you should probably get the kids started on their homework first.

Opening up the mail is enough to make your stomach turn. You remember a time when you looked forward to getting the mail. Not anymore. Today it just contains a notice that your water bill is overdue. That reminds you, you need to get the taxes filed before the deadline.

After the end of a long and taxing day, you sit down on the couch, put your feet up on the table, and turn on the TV. What do you see?

There on the news channel is a politician whose very name raises your blood pressure. He supports some of the most ungodly organizations and unrighteous activities under the sun. He is sporting a three-piece suit that makes your entire wardrobe look like it was purchased at Goodwill. You could sell his watch and make the necessary repairs to your car. "Forget that! I could probably sell that watch and buy a new car!"

"What does this wretched fat-cat know about my life?" you ask. "He makes more than six figures a year, sitting in his air-conditioned office in Washington, DC, sporting about the country in private jets, and eating in high-priced restaurants with political donors. What does he know about the concerns of working men and women? What does he know about the struggles of the middle class?" Frustrated, you change the channel.

It's *Entertainment Tonight*. There on the red carpet stands the beautiful Hollywood couple with the smiles from ear to ear, dressed in nice clothes. Cameras are flashing and fans are cheering. Everyone is fawning over them and wanting their autographs.

Does this couple have kids? Yes, they are in private school with a tutor, getting a stellar education. "I bet they never have to help their kids with their homework." They have time to be at this special event because they have servants who cooked their meal, cleaned up the house, and helped pick out their clothes before they went out that night. In addition, the nanny is at home watching the kids.

Ah, that lucky Hollywood couple. They don't have a care in the world, do they? All the things that plague you and hound your day don't even touch these folks. They got up this morning and their meal was made for them, their house was cleaned by the maid. Their yard was groomed by the landscaper. Their pool was cleaned by the pool cleaner. The nanny ran their kids to school. The staff made their bed and cleaned up their room.

While you were at work, waging the battle for bread, they were working out with a personal trainer, swimming in the pool, reading the newspaper, sitting in the hot tub, and chatting with their agent. After their massage, they found time in their otherwise busy schedule to come out and greet the adoring public.

"I bet they never argue with their spouses. Look at their smiles. They're so happy. They don't have a care in the whole world. And look at his wife. She's beautiful. I bet she wakes up every morning looking like Miss America. I bet her breath smells like a mint garden first thing in the morning. I bet he never has a rough five o'clock shadow or disheveled hair."

How did this ideal couple with the easy life make their millions? They produced and acted in movies that promote ungodly values and destructive behavior. Their films, music, and concerts have featured some of the worst debauchery and godlessness ever to find its way onto a stage. They have given no thought to God. In fact, the only time they take the name of God upon their lips is either to mock Him or to blaspheme His name. These are the wicked! They prosper in their wickedness. They are not in trouble as other men. The concerns that plague the righteous don't land on them. They live above it. They are above the fray.

Charles Spurgeon wrote:

The prosperous wicked escape the killing toils which afflict the mass of mankind; their bread comes to them without care, their wine without stint....Ordinary domestic and personal troubles do not appear to molest them....Fierce trials do not arise to assail them: they smart not under the divine rod. While many saints are both poor and afflicted, the prosperous sinner is neither. He is worse than other men, and yet he is better off; he plows least, and yet has the most fodder. He deserves the hottest hell, and yet has the warmest nest.[6]

Their deaths are easy and carefree. Their lives are easy and carefree. With no troubles or worries, the wicked live their lives and die their deaths without fear or pain. The righteous do not have it so good.

---

6. Spurgeon, 248.

The Problem of "Envy Vision"

Are you starting to feel the weight of what Asaph was describing? Do you feel his perplexity? Are you starting to get a sense of his frustration?

It is easy to see why Asaph was troubled. We know of our own examples. We have seen these very things in our own world and in the headlines all around us. Certainly we can relate.

There is an answer to all of this, but it comes later in the psalm. I don't want to untie this knot for us just yet. We will let Asaph walk us through the solution in due time. We can lighten the load a little bit by recognizing that there are certainly exceptions to Asaph's observations.

I have been speaking in general terms, and almost universal terms, thus far. That is because Asaph speaks in general and universal terms. In these opening verses, Asaph does not seem to be allowing for any exceptions, though I would argue that he certainly would have known of them.

Asaph would not have argued that *every single wicked person without exception* lived an easy life and died an easy death. Likewise, he would not have suggested that *every single righteous person without exception* lacked God's material blessings. Remember, Asaph knew King David. We can all cite exceptions to Asaph's complaints.

During my first year at Bible college, I had a professor whose godliness and intellect were renowned. His name was Herb Peeler. Mr. Peeler was 80 years old and still teaching classes at Millar College of the Bible. Only a few weeks into my first semester, I was sitting in my 8 a.m. class on the Gospel of Matthew, waiting for Mr. Peeler to arrive. One of the other staff members walked in and informed us that Mr. Peeler's classes were canceled. Early that morning, Mrs. Peeler had passed away. Later on we found out the details of Mrs. Peeler's passing.

That morning for the Peelers had been very typical. They woke up early and laid in bed while reading their Bibles together. It was Mr. Peeler's custom to get out of bed and go make a cup of tea for Mrs. Peeler. He would then bring it into the bedroom so she could enjoy a cup of tea in bed while he got ready and then headed off to class. When Mr. Peeler came back into the room with the cup of tea, he found that his wife of more than fifty years had left him for the arms of the Savior. She passed away suddenly, quickly, and quietly after reading the Bible with her husband.

Mr. Peeler eventually passed away thirteen years later. At the age of 93, he was out in the ditch behind his house, burning dead grass. He was healthy and active to the very end. While burning grass, he suddenly, quickly, and quietly dropped dead in the ditch.

They walked with God, and God took them. They are certainly an exception.

Let me offer another from the other side of the ledger. Billionaire Steve Jobs did not pass away quickly or effortlessly. He contracted cancer. That cancer ate away at both his body and his money. One of the last pictures taken of Steve Jobs in public shows that just prior to his death, he was a weak, hollowed-out shell of his former self.

Are there exceptions? Sure there are. There are lots of exceptions. But when our hearts are filled with envy (v. 3), particularly the envy of the arrogant and the wicked, we are unable to see and appreciate those exceptions.

Asaph had "envy vision." His envy of the arrogant distorted his perception of reality and truth. Envy keeps us from seeing real reality. Envy distorts our perception of life as it truly is. When we look at life through glasses of discontent, we only see those things that reinforce our discontentment. When envy resides in the heart, when our hearts are embittered, the only things that we tend to see are the things that feed our envy and inflame our bitterness.

There were exceptions. But Asaph did not see them.

Is it true that *all* the wicked die peacefully? Do *all* the righteous suffer? Are there not righteous who are taken peacefully in their sleep after long, fruitful, and blessed lives filled with days of plenty? And are there not atheists and pagans who died painful, agonizing deaths, wracked with disease and wasting? Surely there are.

There are wicked people who lose their wealth and income and find that their riches have made themselves wings and flown away (Proverbs 23:5). There are a multitude of unrighteous people who find their lives pierced through with many griefs because of their love for money (1 Timothy 6:10). There are righteous and godly people whom the Lord has blessed with riches and wealth and whose wealth has been used for the advancement of God's kingdom. The envious heart cannot see them. To the one with "envy vision," those folks are so rare, so few, they're not even worth considering in the equation.

Do you really think that the Hollywood couple, followed by riches, fame, and fan clubs, really has an ideal home life? Do you really think that they are "not in trouble as other men" (v. 5)? Try following the buzz in Hollywood for one month. It is enough to make your head swim. It is nearly impossible to keep track of who's getting married, who's getting divorced, and who is moving in with whom. Do you really think that such couples enjoy peace at their dining room table? You think that it is all bliss in their bedroom?

How many of them drink themselves to sleep each night because they want to escape their hellish existence? You will never find that out on *Entertainment Tonight* unless they are arrested for a DUI. These arrogant, wicked people, whom we are foolish enough to envy, have to die from drug overdoses, enter rehab centers, or watch their marriages fall apart before we realize that their lives are a living hell.

They struggle with depression, insecurity, and anxiety. They experience loneliness, betrayal, and frustration. Their marriages are not blissful. They have to live with sinners too. Their children fight. They argue with their spouses. They fight over money. They fight over their possessions. Their indulgent lifestyles are merely a salve to soothe an aching conscience and numb their spiritual pain.

Unfortunately, once we catch a glimpse of this reality, our hearts quickly turn to the next shiny object and we envy them.

Asaph's portrayal of reality is not entirely accurate. From Asaph's vantage point, it seemed accurate. He had reached the point where he was hard-pressed not to see this injustice everywhere he turned. All he could see were examples of this inequity. That is the effect of "envy vision."

Asaph needed to get God's perspective. He needed to perceive what was true regarding the arrogant whom he envied. We will get that very same perspective later in the psalm.

3

A Transgressor Abhorred

Psalm 73:6–9
Therefore pride is their necklace;
The garment of violence covers them.
Their eye bulges from fatness;
The imaginations of their heart run riot.
They mock and wickedly speak of oppression;
They speak from on high.
They have set their mouth against the heavens,
And their tongue parades through the earth.

What fills the heart flows from the mouth.

That should be forever enshrined as one of the great "laws" of the universe. Like the laws of Supply and Demand, Gravity, or the Laws of Thermodynamics, this is an undeniable feature of reality. There is a direct link between a man's heart and his mouth.

Jesus said in Matthew 12:33–37:

Either make the tree good and its fruit good, or make the tree bad and its fruit bad; for the tree is known by its fruit. You brood of vipers, how can you, being evil, speak what is good? For the mouth speaks out of that which fills the heart. The good man brings out of his good treasure what is good; and the evil man brings out of his evil treasure what is evil. But I tell you that every careless word that people speak, they shall give an accounting for it in the day of judgment. For by your words you will be justified, and by your words you will be condemned.

If the heart (tree) is filled with blasphemy, the mouth will spill forth blasphemy (fruit). If the heart is filled with pride, the mouth will speak boastful, and arrogant words. Words do not come out of a vacuum. Language expresses the content of the heart. Profane words aren't what makes for a profane man. It is the opposite. A man who is profane, and whose heart is filled with such profanities, will speak profane words.

Jesus said on another occasion, "The good man out of the good treasure of his heart brings forth what is good; and the evil man out of the evil treasure brings forth what is evil; for his mouth speaks from that which fills his heart" (Luke 6:45).

The mouth is like a pressure release valve for the heart. Whatever is inside the heart, when the pressure increases, will come spilling out through the mouth. Our words say a lot about the condition of our heart. That is as sure as gravity.

We see this connection between the heart and mouth in the text which we will be considering in this chapter. In verses 6-9 of the 73rd Psalm, Asaph observed the pride, violence, and abusive speech of the prosperous wicked. The "arrogance" (v. 3) and "pride" (v. 6) that Asaph described inevitably found an outlet in the mocking, oppressive, and blasphemous speech of the prosperous men he envied.

A righteous person should be repulsed by the men described in these verses. Though Asaph envied the prosperity of the wicked, he did not envy their pride. He envied their wealth not their wickedness. The conduct of these prosperous men was abhorrent to Asaph, as it would be to any righteous man. This is what made their prosperity so inexplicable. Why is it that God would grant them such abundant treasure (v. 3) and such an easy life (vv. 4-5)?

If Asaph found the pride, violence, and blasphemous speech of these wicked men so abhorrent, why didn't God? If God *did* find it abhorrent, then why did these men enjoy such wealth?

In verses 6-9, Asaph described the conduct and speech of these reviling blasphemers.

Psalm 73:6
Therefore pride is their necklace;
The garment of violence covers them.

Asaph saw a connection between the arrogant wicked's prosperity and their pride. This is indicated by the connecting conjunctive adverb "therefore." The pride of these arrogant wicked was the result of their prosperity. Their ease of life, comfort in death, and abundant material prosperity only served to puff them up with pride.

It is not difficult to see a connection between the abundance of one's wealth, and the pride of one's heart. How many humble wealthy people do you know? How many people, whose lives are glutted with material prosperity, are truly humble? Sure, they exist, but they are most certainly rare. Material wealth and true humility are only found together in righteous men and women whom God has graced with both material prosperity and a character of humility. The combination of wealth and humility among the wicked is not just rare, it is nonexistent.

True biblical humility is a characteristic created by the Holy Spirit in the heart of a redeemed person who has been crushed by the law and brought to kneel before the cross. It is no surprise that the "arrogant" and the "wicked" (v. 3) wear their pride like a necklace.

This is certainly one of the subtle dangers of material prosperity. Riches have a way of convincing wicked men that they are in some way worthy of the prosperity and comforts they enjoy.

The Wicked Worldview

The wicked have no god to thank but themselves. Refusing to give God glory, they presume that all they have acquired is due to their own hard work, ingenuity, or giftedness. They do not see their abundance as a kindness from God, but rather as the karma they are due. Wicked men recognize no great Benefactor to Whom they owe all the choice comforts they enjoy.

All men instinctively think that some form of karma rules their lot in life. They may not openly admit they believe in karma, but their pride betrays them. They would only take pride in their prosperity if they believed it to be entirely of their own making. Until some grand financial calamity strikes them, they believe they must somehow deserve prosperity, or they would not be enjoying prosperity. They boast as Nebuchadnezzar, "Is this not Babylon the great, which I myself have built as a royal residence by the might of my power and for the glory of my majesty?" (Daniel 4:30).

The wicked instinctively think that all the blessings they have are theirs because they are more deserving or better than those who go without. After all, why would the gods of fate and fortune favor them if they were not eminently favorable?

In America we saw this kind of narcissistic pride unfold before our very eyes in the 2016 presidential race. Donald Trump, a "self-made billionaire" led the top of the Republican ticket almost from the moment he entered the race. Whatever you may think about Donald Trump and his ability to create jobs, cut spending, or make deals with the leaders of other nations, no one can deny that the most dominant aspect of his personality is his pride, arrogance, and narcissism. We were constantly reminded of his abilities, intellect, success, wealth, talents, skill, achievements, and propensity for winning by none other than Donald Trump himself. That is not to suggest that all the other candidates were paragons of Christ-like humility, but the self-promotion of Donald Trump was like something from another world.

This is not unique among the wealthy wicked. It's common. The wicked have no one to credit or thank for their success other than themselves. Eventually, they begin to believe that such blessings of prosperity are owed to them. First, they take credit for their riches, then they feel entitled to their riches.

Open Shame

Unfortunately, their pride is not hidden. Instead, they wear it like a necklace. Asaph employed a clever metaphor to describe the way in which these arrogant and prideful men displayed their pride.

As one might drape a necklace around his neck in order to display it prominently, adorn his dress, and catch the eye of all around, so the prosperous wicked wear their pride openly and unashamedly. They are brazen in their pride. They are narcissistic and arrogant, and do nothing to hide it. They believe they are better than others, and they have no problem saying so. They are proud of their pride. They do not seek humility as a virtue but scorn it as a vice. Their depraved mind views humility as a sign of weakness. They do not see humility as a character quality to be pursued or a virtue to be admired in others. To the arrogant, humility is a shortcoming. To the godly, humility is among the greatest of all virtues.

The condemnation given in Isaiah is certainly fitting for them: "The expression of their faces bears witness against them, and they display their sin like Sodom; they do not even conceal it. Woe to them! For they have brought evil on themselves" (Isaiah 3:9). They are not without pride, but they have a different attitude toward it. The righteous abhor pride not only in others but, first and foremost, in themselves.

Pride is the original sin of the devil (Isaiah 14:12-14; Ezekiel 28:11-19).[1] It has been rightly observed that pride is the mother of every other sin. Rebellion against God is birthed out of a preference for our own will, glory and preeminence. Every sin is a conscious choice of self over God.

For obvious reasons, pride is equally loathsome to God. Proverbs 16:5 says, "Everyone who is proud in heart is an abomination to the Lord; assuredly, he will not be unpunished." Proverbs 21:4: "Haughty eyes and a proud heart, the lamp of the wicked, is sin." That which is an abomination to God is a glory to the wicked. They consider their pride and adornment to be worn for men. They're not ashamed of their arrogance, they flaunt it.

Asaph would've been well served to heed the counsel of Proverbs 16:19: "It is better to be humble in spirit with the lowly than to divide the spoil with the proud." He certainly should not have envied such fools!

Pride is not the only thing they openly flaunt. Asaph says, "The garment of violence covers them." They are so brazen in their arrogance that they even wear violence like a garment.

---

1. These passages are addressed to the King of Babylon and the King of Tyre respectively though both Isaiah and Ezekiel were also speaking of the demonic power behind those earthly kings.

Pride and violence go together. The proud are violent because they think that others are not worth the same respect and dignity as they. They think that others are nothing compared to themselves, and thus can be used or abused for their own ends. This will inevitably lead to violence.

A proud man will use violence to take from others what he deems to be his due. He will use violence to oppress, to exploit, and to abuse others for their own gain. They do not do this in secret. They are open about it. Why should they be ashamed of how they treat others? Others are not worthy of the same respect they deserve, therefore who could possibly think they have done wrong? Remember, first they take credit for their riches, then they feel entitled to their riches. Woe to the person who stands between the prideful man and that to which he believes he is entitled.

The prophet Micah described such workers of iniquity in Micah 2:1–2:

1 Woe to those who scheme iniquity,
　　Who work out evil on their beds!
When morning comes, they do it,
　　For it is in the power of their hands.
2 They covet fields and then seize them,
　　And houses, and take them away.
They rob a man and his house,
　　A man and his inheritance.

Asaph was observing men and women who had become haughty and arrogant. They saw other people as a means to their end and they were not afraid to use violence to achieve that end. Spurgeon said, "They brag and bully, bluster and browbeat, as if they had taken out a license to ride roughshod over all

71

mankind."[2] Asaph envied them. That is a sad commentary on his spiritual condition at the time. Proverbs 3:31: "Do not envy a man of violence and do not choose any of his ways."

A truly humble person does not see others as a means to an end. A truly humble person sees others as more important than themselves. They consider the interests of others ahead of their own (Philippians 2:3-4).

These men displayed their violence in the same manner they displayed their pride, openly and shamelessly. Like one might wear a $10,000 suit or a $50,000 dress to attract attention and make a statement, these prideful, prosperous men and women are willing to display their violence publicly. They gladly wear it in the open like a garment.

They don't fear reprisal. They don't fear public outrage. They don't fear a loss to their reputation or status. Such men do not care what others think of them, for they think enough of themselves. They cannot imagine that anyone thinks any less of them than they do. Their prosperity seems to protect them from insults, from troubles, and from the justice they are due. What a vivid picture!

Psalm 73:7
Their eye bulges from fatness;
The imaginations of their heart run riot.

This is quite a vivid description. The imagery here is graphic. Asaph describes the wicked as those who enjoy such indulgence, glut themselves to such an extreme, that "their eye bulges from fatness." The picture here is of these wicked, so overindulged, they were obese to the point that the fatness of their face

---

2. Charles Haddon Spurgeon, *The Treasury of David*, Vol. 2, *Psalms 58-110* (Peabody: Hendrickson Publishers), 248.

actually distorted their eyes. Their eyes were popping out of their heads from the fatness. When I was a child my grandparents described those who had too much to drink by saying, "Their eyes are floating." That is the imagery. These wicked had so much to eat their eyes bulged out of their head.

In Asaph's time, obesity was anything but an epidemic. Most people fought the battle for bread on a daily basis, struggling just to put another meal on the table. There were not many people that were afforded the luxury of overeating. It was radically different than what we are familiar with in our own country.

The vast majority of people in the United States live with an abundance that most of the world, and most of world history, has never known. Solomon, in all his glory, did not enjoy the most meager of my modern conveniences. Solomon could not touch a button and adjust the climate in his home to within a couple of degrees. Solomon could not turn a handle and have at his disposal an unlimited amount of fresh, clean, warm and cold water. Solomon could not communicate with his friends and family half a world away effortlessly and freely. Today I live at a level of comfort that was unknown to the greatest kings of the world. I am by no means rich. I'm average.

Further, most of the world has no idea what it is like to have a pantry full of food. They can't imagine what it is like to have a freezer full of meat, a refrigerator full of fresh produce, and cupboards full of canned goods. In fact, most of the world has no idea what a "leftover" is. My children know what leftovers are, and they complain every time they have to heat one up in the microwave - another little device that would make Solomon jealous.

We live in a land and time of great abundance and great indulgence. Not only do we know what it is like to have an abundant provision, we know what it is like to have an indulgent provision. Asaph could not imagine the daily choices and provision of food which we take for granted. It seemed to him that the wicked always had more than enough.

While the righteous go without, the wicked are glutted. While the righteous are lucky to enjoy one feast a year, the wicked seem to run on an unending string of feasts and gluttonous indulgences. While those who feared God had barely enough to live, those who hated God satiated themselves with the most fattening, the most ostentatious, the most abundant feasts imaginable. What an injustice!

And to go further, when it came to indulgence, "the imaginations of their heart [ran] riot." Whatever their heart desired, they enjoyed. Whatever their imagination could dream up, they had it.

It does not matter how ostentatious or extravagant the expense, it seems that the prosperous wicked are able to enjoy it. If they wish it, they get it. Their greediness is exceeded by their indulgence. It's not just that they have enough while others may go without, but they have more than enough. They can afford to spare no expense, to lavish on themselves, to their own comfort and convenience, any earthly pleasure or any physical enjoyment they can imagine.

We can all think of modern-day examples of the wicked doing the same thing today. Christians in Iran sit in prison and live on meager crumbs while the Mullah's live in palaces and enjoy feasts of epic proportions. The leader of North Korea starves his citizens while parading his own fattened face on every billboard in the country. His eye bulges from his fatness.

Most of the prosperous wicked in our own day waste more food than my family eats. In fact, they waste more resources than most of us can imagine. While giving no thought or thanks to God, they enjoy wealth and prosperity we can only dream about. They are the wicked, the arrogant, the prideful and violent.

It is the sinfulness and wickedness of these prosperous people that so vexed Asaph. He didn't lament that David enjoyed wealth, nor did he decry the treasure enjoyed by the righteous. The grand inequity rested with the fact that such treasure belonged to those filled with pride and violence.

It is important to recognize that the issue was not the existence or use of wealth. Asaph was not lamenting that people enjoy such prosperity. It is not the prosperity that is inherently sinful or wicked. What confounded Asaph was the fact that it appeared such prosperity rested almost entirely in the hands of those who deserved it least.

The Bible does not teach that being rich is a sin. Abraham was wealthy (Genesis 13:2). Job and David were wealthy (Job 1:3; 1 Chronicles 29:3-5). Joseph of Arimathea was wealthy (Matthew 27:57). There were righteous and godly people in Scripture to whom God blessed with riches and wealth (Proverbs 10:22). We should not for one moment think that Asaph's lament would place him comfortably in the Occupy Wall Street Movement crying out against the "1%" and selfishly demanding government redistribution of wealth in the spirit of a Bernie Sanders revolution. Asaph was no liberal social justice warrior lamenting the freedom of others to use their resources as they saw fit. It is the wickedness of these men and women who enjoyed such blessings that perplexed Asaph. It was not the existence of prosperity that was the problem, it was the wickedness of the men in whose hands it rested.

How was it possible that God, Who is good to His people - to those who are pure in heart - could give to men such as this so much wealth? Why would God tolerate such lascivious men enjoying all that luxury?

The Terrible Tongue of the Prosperous Wicked

Psalm 73:8
They mock and wickedly speak of oppression;
They speak from on high.

It is nearly impossible to get a prideful man to shut his mouth. One distinguishing characteristic of a man who wears pride like a necklace is his ability to speak endlessly of himself: his own accomplishments, achievements, and wisdom. The wicked man believes he has himself to thank for his riches and so he talks endlessly about himself.

Not only is the speech of the wicked self-centered and self-aggrandizing, but it is characteristically arrogantly opposed to God. Any man or woman who seeks to make themselves look great must first make any and all rivals look small. The prideful man can tolerate no competitors. His mouth will serve as the vent for the prideful filth that fills his heart.

Jesus candidly spoke of the connection between the contents of our heart and the words of our mouth. He condemned the Pharisees with these words in Matthew 12:34–37:

> You brood of vipers, how can you, being evil, speak what is good? For the mouth speaks out of that which fills the heart. The good man brings out of his good treasure what is good; and the evil man brings out of his evil treasure what is evil. But I tell you that every careless word that people speak, they shall give an accounting for it in the day of judgment. For by your words you will be justified, and by your words you will be condemned.[3]

---

3. See also Luke 6:45.

It is no surprise that Asaph would describe the speech of these prosperous fools. We would expect that the pride that filled their hearts would spew forth from their mouths and it most certainly did.

From verse 8 we can see three things that characterize their speech.

First, their speech is marked by mockery. The prosperous proud do not honor God with their lips, but mock Him. Rather than using their tongue to praise God - to honor Him, the Giver of every good gift (James 1:17) - they use their mouth to mock God and His truth. They will not use their tongue to "declare [God's] righteousness and [His] praise all day long" (Psalm 35:28). Their pride will not allow them to give glory to another. They must have all glory for themselves. They mock God instead. "The mouth of the righteous utters wisdom, and his tongue speaks justice" (Psalm 37:30), but the mouth of a fool is given to the mockery of all that the righteous hold dear.

Nothing has changed. In our own day, Christians are routinely mocked on television, in the news, and among the elites. In fact, Christians, the Christian religion, the Bible, and the true God are the only things that can be mocked with impunity. If any news anchor even once treated Islam with the same disrespect they show toward Christianity on a routine basis, they would be fired, pilloried, and banned from ever working for any news outlet ever again.

The word of God is mocked in every state-run educational facility from kindergarten to graduate school. Bill Maher routinely attacks Christians and the Bible, and he makes millions of dollars doing it. Bill Nye, The Science Guy, is a celebrity sensation in large part because of his open opposition to Christian theism and the doctrine of creation. As recent as 2015, he openly mocked the pro-life camp and Christians who base their morality on the Bible.

Jesus said this would be the case. He warned His disciples in John 15:18–25:

> If the world hates you, you know that it has hated Me before it hated you. If you were of the world, the world would love its own; but because you are not of the world, but I chose you out of the world, because of this the world hates you. Remember the word that I said to you, "A slave is not greater than his master." If they persecuted Me, they will also persecute you; if they kept My word, they will keep yours also. But all these things they will do to you for My name's sake, because they do not know the One who sent Me. If I had not come and spoken to them, they would not have sin, but now they have no excuse for their sin. He who hates Me hates My Father also. If I had not done among them the works which no one else did, they would not have sin; but now they have both seen and hated Me and My Father as well. But they have done this to fulfill the word that is written in their Law, "THEY HATED ME WITHOUT A CAUSE."

Though the world's hatred for the Light should not take us by surprise, it can be discouraging to observe them prospering from that hatred. I would never deny anyone the right to believe what they want or to speak as they wish regarding their beliefs, but I can certainly sympathize with Asaph's frustration from watching such mockers enjoy a free pass to ride the gravy train of life.

Second, their speech is violent. They "wickedly speak of oppression." Having gained much of their wealth through open violence, they now boast of such oppression. It is not enough for them to oppress others as a matter of course, but they boast of such oppression. They gloat of their abuse of others. They plan their oppression. They delight in these things and speaking of their oppressive, abusive, and violent ways is second nature to them. They see nothing wrong with abusing people for their own ends.

Spurgeon writes:

> They choose oppression as their subject, and they not only defend it, but advocate it, glory in it, and would feign make it the general rule among all nations....Indeed, we see that wicked men, after having for some time got everything to prosper according to their desires, cast off all shame, and are at no pains to conceal themselves, when about to commit iniquity, but loudly proclaim their own turpitude.[4]

Hitler spoke openly of his "final solution." He did not hide his intentions, his evil machinations, or his murderous plans. He was brazenly open about his acts of oppression and violence. He prospered in them, at least for a time.

In 2015, a series of undercover videos were released by the Center for Medical Progress exposing the horrors of the abortion industry.[5] In those videos, Planned Parenthood executives openly discussed methods of murdering unborn children for the purpose of maximizing profits from the sale of undamaged organs and tissues. This they do while sipping wine and eating a salad in a classy restaurant. In one disturbing video, a Planned Parenthood executive coldly remarks, "I want a Lamborghini." They wickedly speak of oppression. These are the wicked, increasing in wealth!

---

4. Turpitude means "a vile, shameful, or base character; depravity; a vile or depraved act." Spurgeon, 248 & 260.
5. http://www.centerformedicalprogress.org/

The arrogant, prosperous wicked blithely describe their exploitation of others. They speak openly of how they use the laws to benefit themselves and how they buy favors and influence among the rich and powerful. They will speak without shame concerning how they have used, abused, and exploited others for their own personal gain. They mock and wickedly speak of oppression.

Third, their speech is prideful and condescending. As Asaph says, "They speak from on high."

Have you ever had the misfortune to spend a great deal of time with someone who can never utter the words "I don't know." These are people who know everything about everything. No matter what subject, they speak as if they are experts. No matter what field of knowledge is at the center of the conversation, this person has been there, done that, and is an expert on all things related to it. Though such a cocky self-assurance may initially cause people to think they are well-read, proficient conversationalists, it eventually wears quite thin. People begin to catch on to the game. Eventually their expertise in every field starts to sound rather boorish and puerile.

Those who wear pride like a necklace also speak as if they were someone great. They style themselves as a modern E.F. Hutton imagining people around them hushing their own conversations to hear theirs. They arrogantly assume that everyone is waiting with bated breath, hanging on every word for their wisdom from on high.

These men exalt themselves as if they are speaking the very words of God. They talk as if they have authority and people are obligated to listen to them. They vainly imagine they have solutions for the problems that ail us all. They speak as if they are the dispensers of wisdom on life, happiness, prosperity, eternity, and the issues facing our nations.

The 24-hour news cycle is filled with talking heads pontificating on subjects they know nothing about on an endless loop that would make the creators of the movie *Groundhog Day* jealous. This combination of media elitists, political ruling class experts, and "contributors" is what passes for news. These are the experts who "speak from on high."

Consider the arrogance of our overlords who expect us to obey the edicts of the Supreme Court justices as if these men and women speak the very oracles of God. This collection of largely irreligious men and women imbued with worldly, satanic wisdom "hand down" their decisions as if they are divine decrees. We are all told to get in line and follow along quietly. They speak from on high.

Scripture says, "The fear of the Lord is the beginning of knowledge; fools despise wisdom and instruction" (Proverbs 1:7), and, "The fear of the Lord is the beginning of wisdom, and the knowledge of the Holy One is understanding" (Proverbs 9:10). True wisdom and true knowledge are available only to the righteous who fear the Lord and submit to His wisdom and revelation of truth. There is more true wisdom and knowledge in the heart of one poor righteous beggar who knows God's Word and fears God than there is in all the earthly magistrates, Supreme Court justices, and media talking heads combined. Spurgeon wrote:

> Their high heads, like tall chimneys, vomit black smoke. Big talk streams from them, their language is colossal, their magniloquence ridiculous. They are Sir Oracle in every case, they speak as from the judge's bench, and expect all the world to stand in awe of them.[6]

---

6. Spurgeon, 248.

A Parade of Tongues

Psalm 73:9

They have set their mouth against the heavens,
And their tongue parades through the earth.

The prosperous wicked demonstrate their insolence by aiming their speech against Heaven itself. They are not content to abuse men with their words, but find it necessary to aim their barbs at God as well. Pride makes them God's enemy, their mouth His abusers.

Though these prosperous fools should be bowing down to give God thanks for every last blessing they enjoy, instead they shake their fist at God and hurl abusive accusations and blasphemies against Him. Truly, "'Their throat is an open grave, With their tongues they keep deceiving,' 'The poison of asps is under their lips'; 'Whose mouth is full of cursing and bitterness'" (Romans 3:13–14).

God, the giver of every good thing they have enjoyed, receives nothing but abuse and blasphemies from them. He is the object of their white-hot hatred. If given the opportunity and the means, they would reach into Heaven and shake God's throne with such violence as to unseat Him from it. They speak lies to assault the God of truth. They speak darkness to cloud the light of revelation. They slander the God who is infinitely worthy of their praise and adoration.

It is not surprising that unbelievers speak like this, but it is unnerving to see them prosper in it. Again, this is the heart of Asaph's complaint. I expect wicked and unregenerate men and women to blaspheme God. I expect them to vent their hatred and the darkness of their heart through their words. What we do not expect is that they should profit so handsomely from their rebellion, and that God should permit that prosperity.

Why does God allow Richard Dawkins, Sam Harris, Christopher Hitchens, and Daniel Dennett (collectively known as "The Four Horsemen of New Atheism"), to receive such abundant treasure from their atheistic campaigns? These men spend their days fighting against God in whom they do not believe. They make millions of dollars presenting atheistic arguments, slandering the God of the Bible, and attacking Christian theism. Why should riches and honor, blessings and treasures, be the lot of men who have "set their mouth against the heavens"?

Further, why should their wicked speech enjoy such free course? We might hope that God would limit the effects of their blasphemous diatribes. Instead, their wicked, abusive speech spreads like gangrene through the earth.

The imagery used by Asaph is really quite vivid. Imagine a tongue walking on legs with its head held high, strutting throughout the earth unhindered. With all the pomposity and presumption which we might expect from the mouth of the prosperous wicked, their tongues strut through city after city, town after town, and village after village. Their tongue spreads lies, deceit, and vile speech. They prosper for it.

The righteous long for the day when "the earth will be full of the knowledge of the LORD as the waters cover the sea" (Isaiah 11:9) and it grieves the soul of the righteous to see God's name blasphemed in every corner of the world. Yet, lamentably, it seems that the more abusive the speech or the more devious the lie, the greater that cancer is spread. There is no end to their words and no limit to their influence.

We live in an age where such "parading" is more possible than ever before. Asaph could never have dreamed of the day when the blasphemous lies of the prosperity gospel, the charismatic deception, and the New Apostolic Reformation could be instantly transmitted from Houston Texas to Nairobi. Today, the arrogant tongue of Creflo Dollar is filmed in Anytown, USA, and instantly beamed via satellite to the remotest village in Asia. Internet, radio, television, and the cheap access to all forms of mass media give a platform to the blasphemous lies of wicked fools that previous generations could have never imagined. Their tongue parades through the earth.

Further, the ungodly worldview promoted in American culture and propagated through Hollywood's drivel, finds a receptive audience in nearly every nation on the planet. The same mass media that allows the faithful pastor in Podunk, Nebraska to have his expository sermon heard around the world also allows the atheistic, God-hating blasphemies of those who "set their mouth against the heavens" to parade through the earth. Which one do you think gets the most press? There is an old adage that says, "A lie can travel halfway around the world while the truth is putting on its shoes."[7]

Can You Relate?

Not only can you sense Asaph's frustration but you can probably relate to it. Don't you wish that the wisdom and worldview of righteous men would dominate in public discourse? Don't you wish the airwaves, the media, and culture were permeated with the true knowledge of God instead of the lies and blasphemies perpetuated by the wicked? Doesn't it seem as if life would be better, people would be better off, and the world would be a better place to live, if righteous men had the wealth and treasure that is currently enjoyed by the arrogant? Don't you sometimes feel that the wealth of this world is enjoyed by all the wrong people?

---

7. Though that quote is often attributed to Mark Twain, no one is certain where the adage originated. It has appeared for hundreds of years in various forms.

Asaph did. He found himself envying for one reason the very reprobates he despised for another. Truly, his "steps had almost slipped." If we don't have God's perspective on the wicked and their riches, we can easily fall into the same trap.

We will get to that perspective in time (v. 15ff.), but first we must look at a treachery approved. That is the next chapter.

4

A Treachery Approved

Psalm 73:10-12
Therefore his people return to this place,
And waters of abundance are drunk by them.
They say, "How does God know?
And is there knowledge with the Most High?"
Behold, these are the wicked;
And always at ease, they have increased in wealth.

Thought experiment: imagine a "physical conscience" were built into human physiology. Imagine every time someone told a lie, their mouth and throat would immediately begin to burn with unrelenting and tormenting pain as if they had ingested a handful of Carolina Reaper peppers.[1] Further imagine that this unrelenting pain would last for one hour and then subside.

Oh, how life would be different! Do you think trying court cases would be easier and quicker? How much shorter would news broadcasts and commercials be? The political roundtable

---

[1]. The Carolina Reaper is said to be the hottest pepper in the world. It has a SHU (Scoville Heat Unit) rating of 2,200,000. The Ghost Pepper ranks #7 at 1,041,427. https://www.crazyhotseeds.com/top-10-worlds-hottest-peppers/

discussions on your favorite cable news channel would sound a lot different. Sorting out arguments between your kids might be enjoyable! How fun would it be to watch the televangelists on TBN?

How often would you lie? How often would you be tempted to lie? How closely would you evaluate every statement you made for accuracy and precision before uttering it?

The allure of dishonesty is much greater when we believe we have a good chance of "getting away with it." We are much more willing to engage in wicked behavior if the consequences of our behavior are not immediate. An immoral man views pornography or commits adultery because he has convinced himself that he can avoid the consequences of his sin. He believes that his wife will never find out. He is convinced the day of reckoning will never come.

When I was young I used to abuse my body with reckless abandon. I would regularly climb trees and jump out, jump off the roof of our house or out the loft of my grandparents' barn. Whether I was swimming, riding my bike, hitching a ride on a train, or jumping from some structure, I was careless to the point of stupidity.

My older relatives used to warn me: "You're going to regret doing that when you get to be about 40 years old!" or, "You'll feel that when you get older."

Older?! I never planned on getting older. 40? That was, like, FOREVER from now! It could never be as bad as everyone said, right? I would be the guy who escaped the consequences. Suffering later was not guaranteed and so I was willing to risk it.

Forty came much more quickly than I ever imagined it would. As it turns out, my older relatives' warnings were virtually prophetic in their accuracy! If I had a DeLorean time machine, I would go back to 1984 and slap myself and tell myself to smarten up!

The more distance there is between our actions and the consequences of our actions, the easier it is to convince ourselves that those consequences can be avoided. Solomon stated that principle this way: "Because the sentence against an evil deed is not executed quickly, therefore the hearts of the sons of men among them are given fully to do evil" (Ecclesiastes 8:11). When justice is delayed, evil is incentivized.

Parents understand how this principle works with their children. When a mother says the words, "You just wait till your father gets home!" the child hears, "I will probably forget all about this by the time your father gets home!"

In the civil realm[2] we see the truthfulness of Solomon's observation played out in our headlines each and every day. A man who commits a violent crime spends years waiting for justice. The investigation, trials, and appeals can take decades to work their way through the "justice system" before a sentence is handed down. The wheels of justice grind slowly, if at all. The consequences of this are plain for all to see. The hearts of the sons of men in our own nation are fully set to do evil.

When consequences come slowly, evil is incentivized. The more disconnected the punishment from the crime, the more crime is encouraged. So it is with the conduct of the wicked. The prosperous wicked grow bold in their irreverence and godlessness. They become hardened in their rebellion as each passing day brings prosperity in their sin instead of punishment for their sin.

They begin to reason that God must be unconcerned with, if not unaware of, their sin. They say, "How does God know? And is

---

2. It is the realm of civil government and its execution of justice for crime that Solomon is primarily addressing in the text.

there knowledge with the Most High?" (Psalm 73:11). When the wicked do not face any immediate divine justice for their pride, violence, mockery, oppression, and insolent speech, they start to question whether there will EVER be any such consequences. After all, they reason, "Is there knowledge with the Most High?"

A Problem Passage

Verses 10-12 of this psalm present a very difficult interpretive challenge. A search of a half-dozen commentaries will likely turn up at least as many possible interpretations. As Spurgeon says regarding verse 10, "It seems impossible to ascertain with any degree of precision, the meaning of this verse, or to whom it relates."[3]

With challenging passages of Scripture, we can sometimes arrive at the correct interpretation by ruling out other possibilities. Say for instance there are four possible interpretations of a passage. We could likely rule out three of them by running the options through a series of questions:

1. Does this interpretation fit with the context?

2. Does this interpretation fit with the flow of argument/narrative being presented by the author?

3. Does this interpretation fit with other passages of Scripture?

Any possible interpretation of a passage that does not fit the context, the author's argument in that context, or the doctrine found in the rest of Scripture, certainly cannot be the right

---

3. Charles Haddon Spurgeon, *The Treasury of David*, Vol. 2, *Psalms 58-110* (Peabody: Hendrickson Publishers), 260.

interpretation. In the case of Psalm 73:10-12, even after running the verses through this tight interpretive grid, we are still left with several good, viable, possible understandings of the passage.

Consider the different interpretive possibilities presented by the following verses.

Psalm 73:10
Therefore his people return to this place,
And waters of abundance are drunk by them.

Questions:

1. Who are "his people"? Does this describe the people of God who remain faithful to God? Does this refer to apostate "God fearers" whose feet slip (v. 2) and join the wicked? Or are these the people who have joined the cause of the prosperous wicked? Does it describe those men and women who surround the wicked and approve of their rebellion?

2. What is "this place"? Some suggest it refers to the temple. Some say it refers to the "place of lament," meaning that these people (whoever they are) eventually come to "this place" of decrying the prosperity of the wicked as Asaph has been doing in this psalm. Some say "this place" refers to the side of the wicked, meaning they come to join the cause of the wicked. Or, "this place" could refer to the place of stumbling over the prosperity of the wicked as Asaph nearly did (v. 2).

3. What are "waters of abundance"? This could be a figure of speech for a cup of wrath meaning that "his people" (the people allied with the wicked) drink the full cup of God's wrath for their sin. It could refer to literal water meaning these people get some form of refreshment. It might refer figuratively to tears, meaning

that the result of joining the cause of the wicked is that "his people" end up drinking their own tears.

4. What does the word "drunk" mean? This word can refer to "drinking deeply," "drinking dry," "being drained out," or "being squeezed out." This word can actually mean to "wring out, i.e., pressing motions of the hands on moisture-holding fabric to take the moisture out" (Judges 6:38).[4] So does the word refer to drinking these "waters of abundance" or to wringing them out of something or someone else?

5. Who is "them"? Does this refer to the prosperous wicked, their followers, the people of God, or apostates who leave the fear of God to join the wicked?

As you can see, discerning Asaph's intention is very difficult. A mix and match of the above options yield quite a diverse selection of meanings. Granted, not all of them are equally valid, but several of them are. You can get a sense of the variety of ways the verse can be understood by looking at how different translations render the text.

> KJV: Therefore his people return hither:
> And waters of a full cup are wrung out to them.

> NKJV: Therefore his people return here,
> And waters of a full cup are drained by them.

> NIV: Therefore their people turn to them
> and drink up waters in abundance.

---

4. J. Swanson, *Dictionary of Biblical Languages with Semantic Domains : Hebrew (Old Testament)* (electronic ed.). Oak Harbor: Logos Research Systems, Inc., 1997.

ESV: Therefore his people turn back to them,
   and find no fault in them.

NASB: Therefore his people return to this place,
   And waters of abundance are drunk by them.

Verse 11 presents a couple more questions.

Psalm 73:11
They say, "How does God know?
And is there knowledge with the Most High?"

1. Who is "they" referring to? Does this refer to "his people" mentioned in the previous verse or to those who get the "waters of abundance"? Or does this refer to the "wicked" mentioned in the next verse, verse 12?

2. Who is it that is questioning the knowledge of the Most High? Is this the wicked (v. 12) who are emboldened in their sin because God seems unobservant of their ways? Or is this the righteous that are wondering if God sees their suffering and oppression?

It is entirely possible that the intended meaning of Asaph cannot be known by us with any certainty at all. After all, verse 10 could be a proverb, a figure of speech, a metaphor, or a veiled reference to a cultural icon, the meaning of which was known by everyone in Asaph's day but is lost to us after 3,000 years.

Imagine that I were to write a short article about one of our most recent election cycles and I were to describe it as "a contest for power between two political parties brought to you by House of Cards and Game of Thrones."[5] Everyone reading those words today understands the cultural references to two television programs, but you can imagine the confusion that might ensue 3,000 years from now as readers try to discern my meaning. From a radically different culture, without any knowledge of our context, the full import of my words would be entirely lost on them. That may be what we are dealing with in verse 10.

Most Likely Meanings

We can narrow down the list of possibilities to a few meanings that best fit the context. We can arrange the possibilities under three headings. These verses describe either:

* The lament of God's people,

* The refreshment of God's people, or

* The apostasy of God's people.

These are the ways commentators have commonly understood these words of Asaph.

The Lament of God's People

Option #1: Asaph is describing God's people lamenting their treatment at the hands of the prosperous wicked. God's people come to the temple with their complaint. They come to the sanctuary of God (v. 17) where they cry out abundant tears over their own chastening and difficult life (v. 14) and express their perplexity over the wealth enjoyed by the ungodly. These

---

5. Just to be clear, I, Jim Osman, have never seen a single episode of either of these programs. Nor is this in any way a recommendation for them. The reference to these cultural phenomes is for illustrative purposes only.

righteous ones even start to wonder if God knows of their difficulties (v. 11), since He appears to be apathetic to the rebellion and increasing wealth of these prosperous wicked (v. 12).

The easy life and prosperity of the wicked can be a cause of great distress for the righteous. How many a righteous man or woman has cried before God over the affliction they suffer while their ungodly pagan neighbor eases through life with nary a care? Far too many! Without God's perspective on the prosperity of the wicked, the righteous even begin to question whether God truly knows what they are going through. How can He be silent in the face of such inequity? Does He see our abundant tears as they are wrung out before Him?

This doubting of God's knowledge and goodness is the very slipping of feet that Asaph described in verse 2: "But as for me, my feet came close to stumbling, my steps had almost slipped." Because of the wealth enjoyed by the wicked (vv. 3-5) in spite of their grievous sin (vv. 6-9), the righteous cry out to God and wonder if He sees and cares (vv. 10-12).

Option #2: Asaph is describing God's people lamenting God's seeming indifference. According to this view, verse 10 describes God's people coming to the temple crying tears in abundance. Verse 11 is taken to be the words of the righteous who begin wondering if there is "knowledge with the Most High." This view is similar to the first view with the exception that it is not their treatment at the hand of the wicked that the righteous lament, but God's apparent indifference to that treatment.

There may have been some in the nation of Israel whose feet almost slipped (v. 2), not because they were envious of the prosperous wicked, but because they began to doubt God's knowledge and care in the face of that prosperity and their own affliction. They reflected on their own affliction (v. 14) and began to question the profit of serving God (v. 14).

Option #3: Asaph is describing God's people lamenting the prosperity of the wicked. As with the other views, this one fits the context. According to this view, Asaph is among "His people" who come again to the temple crying abundant tears to lament God's apparent blessing on the wicked. Verses 1-9 have recorded Asaph's lament, and now he is joined by others who share his distress. Verse 11 would describe the wicked who taunt the righteous by suggesting that God is ignorant of their cries, their suffering, and/or the oppressive deeds of the wicked.

Option #4: Asaph is describing how the prosperous wicked treat the righteous. This view takes "His people" to refer to "God's people" and "this place" to refer to being under the power of the wicked.

Asaph had just described how these prosperous wicked are characterized by violence and pride (v. 6), as well as mockery and oppression (v. 8). Therefore, Asaph may be describing the treatment the righteous receive at their hands. The "waters of abundance" would describe the tears of the righteous as they are wrung out of them in fullest measure by the oppressive hand of the wicked. The sorrows of the righteous "are as full as the wicked man's prosperity."[6] They start to wonder if God is ignorant of their oppression (v. 11) since the oppression of the righteous by the wicked only served to increase their wealth (v. 12). We can all think of examples of the righteous being oppressed while the impenitent continue in their rebellion and prosper by it.

Spurgeon quotes a Mr. Mudge who takes verse 10 to mean: "Should God's people fall into their [the wicked] hands, they

---

6. Spurgeon, 249.

would squeeze them to the full, they would wring out all the juice out of their bodies."[7]

The Refreshment of God's People

Option #5: Asaph is describing the refreshment that God's people receive when they come to the temple for worship and perspective.

According to this view, God's people come to the temple where they receive the waters of refreshment in abundance (v. 10). It is in the temple, in the sanctuary of God, where Asaph gained a new perspective on the prosperity enjoyed by the wicked (vv. 16-17). His new perspective described in verses 18-28 would have been a welcome refreshment to his otherwise parched soul. In our worship and fellowship with the people of God, we are edified, equipped, and encouraged. We are continually spiritually refreshed as we draw near to God in worship.

The main problem with this interpretation is the fact that it tends to view verse 10 as a very isolated thought. Verse 11 continues with describing the wicked and their denial of God's knowledge of their deeds and verse 12 exclaims, "These are the wicked!" If verse 10 is describing the refreshment gained by the righteous in worship, it would be far more natural for Asaph to say this down in verses 15-17. In other words, the thought would seem very out of place.

The Apostasy of God's People

Option #6: Asaph is describing how the righteous are lured away by the prosperity of the wicked. According to this view, when righteous men and women observe the prosperity of the

---

7. Ibid., 260.

wicked (v. 2), they are lured away from the paths of righteousness to join the cause of the wicked in hopes of sharing in that prosperity. Like Asaph, these righteous people begin to question whether they have "kept their heart pure" and "washed their hands in innocence" for nothing (v. 13). After all, they might reason, "What does righteousness profit when the wicked are profiting?"

Verse 10 is understood as describing the people of God (His people) who come to the side of the wicked. "This place" would refer to the place of the self-indulgent, arrogant mockers described in the previous verses (vv. 4-9).

As the righteous apostatize and leave the paths of righteousness for the profits of wickedness, they begin to drink in the abundance that is enjoyed by the wicked. "Waters of abundance are drunk by them."

Alternately, the "waters of abundance drunk by them" is sometimes understood to refer to the tears the righteous shed because of their apostasy. As a result of joining the cause of the wicked, the righteous do not receive abundant prosperity. Instead, their apostasy only brings them "tears of abundance" as they are further exploited by the wicked. In other words, the apostasy of the righteous brings them no benefit, only further suffering.

So Many Choices

I realize I have just presented you with a lot of options. All these interpretations fit the context. All of them are theologically sound. With the possible exception of option #5, all of them fit the flow of thought in this psalm. If I had to choose one of them, option #6 appears to fit best.

If Asaph was envious of the prosperity (v. 3), we can be certain that others were as well. He would not have been the only one to wonder if maintaining a pure heart and clean hands (v. 13) was really worth the effort in light of the discipline the righteous endured (v. 14) and their oppression at the hands of wicked men (v. 6). It is not difficult to imagine that many who were tempted by the wicked did not just come "close to stumbling," but actually fell. For many, the temptation would prove too great.

Remember the Apostle Paul's warning:

> Those who want to get rich fall into temptation and a snare and many foolish and harmful desires which plunge men into ruin and destruction. For the love of money is a root of all sorts of evil, and some by longing for it have wandered away from the faith and pierced themselves with many griefs. (1 Timothy 6:9–10)

This was not just a danger in New Testament times. If the lust for gold motivates apostasy in our own day, we can safely assume the same would be true in Asaph's (Jude 11, 16; 2 Peter 2:2-3, 15).

It would have been very disheartening for Asaph to watch a number of his friends or even family members abandon the pursuit of holiness to align themselves with the prosperous wicked. Imagine the pain of watching on as those you love slowly leave the path of righteousness to pursue lives of ease and comfort. This would cause added vexation for Asaph in his already difficult struggle to walk the narrow path.

Asaph would have to watch the ranks of the wicked swell as the number of truly righteous dwindled. He would even begin to fear that eventually he might stand alone. If we have learned anything from our experiences in modern American culture, it is this: the more public opinion turns in favor of wickedness, the more emboldened the wicked get. Psalm 12:8 says, "The wicked strut about on every side when vileness is exalted among the sons of men."

If Asaph was witnessing a large-scale abandonment of truth for the easy and prosperous path of least resistance, he would've found himself in a very awkward position. Asaph would have known that compromising was out of the question yet he would have found himself increasingly tempted to do so. The thought of joining the wicked is both alluring and revolting at the same time. While envying their easy life, Asaph would be repulsed by the thought of falling away from truth. Yet as the number of the wicked swelled, his vexation would only increase. Such is the lot of the truly righteous ones.

Does God Know?

Psalm 73:11
**They say, "How does God know?
And is there knowledge with the Most High?"**

If verse 10 is describing the apostasy of Israelites, then verse 11 either records the words of the apostates or the words of the prosperous wicked. Since verse 12 begins, "Behold, these are the wicked," it seems best to take these as the words of the wicked that Asaph described in vv. 3-9, rather than the apostates mentioned in verse 10.

These words do sound as if they come from the lips of wicked people. These men question whether God truly knows of their crimes.[8] Their denial of God's omniscience is also a denial of ultimate justice. For if God does not know about their wicked deeds, then they will not have to face punishment for them.

---

8. I wrote a series of articles on Open Theism refuting the errors of those who deny the omniscience of God. These articles are available at our website: kootenaichurch.org.

When wicked men prosper in their wickedness, they begin to reason that God either does not know of their treachery, or, if He does know, He does not care. Either way, they figure that they will get away with their wickedness. If God does not know, then He certainly cannot ever punish them for it. If God does not care, then he certainly will not ever punish them for it. When justice is delayed, evil is incentivized. If they have faced no retribution for their oppression in this life, why should they expect one in the life to come? If God knows of their wickedness, why have they seemingly been rewarded for it with riches and prosperity in this world? If God cares about their wickedness, why does He appear to turn a blind eye to it in this life? The fact that the wicked prosper is interpreted by the wicked to mean that God does not know or care about their wickedness.

Believers need to beware of falling into the same trap. It is the path of many small compromises that leads to a giant fall at the end. Such a fall begins with one small lie, one small look at pornography, or one small moral compromise. The whirlwind of those seeds sown is not felt immediately. We begin to reason that these small sins must not matter to God since we face no immediate consequences for them.

This is followed by the temptation to tell another lie, steal another look, and compromise a little bit more. The lack of immediate consequences convinces us that either God has turned His eyes away from our indiscretions or they have somehow passed below His radar. We end up running an ever-broadening course of compromises convincing ourselves that God does not see, does not care, and does not know.

Finally, we reap the whirlwind.

Psalm 73:12
Behold, these are the wicked;
And always at ease, they have increased in wealth.

This is the last positive thing said about the wicked or their wealth in this psalm. This is Asaph's closing description of the prosperous wicked and it sums up his previous lament wonderfully.

Behold the wicked! Let your eyes gaze upon them! They are a spectacle worth viewing. Have you ever seen such a thing? Have you ever seen somebody so undeserving of riches? Have you ever seen somebody so deserving of God's judgment? Look at it! Our eyes can hardly believe what we see!

We observe men clothed in wickedness and riches. They live a comfortable life. They have nothing but plenty. They have ease and convenience. Somehow they avoid all the toils and foibles that make life so mundane and vexing for the rest of us. These who deserve the wrath of God die in peace. What an injustice! Look at it! BEHOLD IT!!! Look at this great stumbling block to faith.

If it is not enough just to look upon what Asaph has described, consider this closing statement regarding their prosperity: "They have increased in wealth." Asaph laments not only that they are wealthy, but that they increase in wealth.

It would be bad enough if the wicked had achieved a level of wealth at some point in the past that was maintained in spite of their wickedness. It is worse that while continuing in their wickedness, the wealth continues to increase. This is a double insult!

This is the opposite of what we would hope to see. Our sense of righteous justice tells us that the wicked described by Asaph should not even have blessings in this life, let alone see them increase. We would want to see anti-God agendas defunded. Instead, those programs that destroy people, promote immorality, and oppose God's truth seem to never lack for financial support.

On August 23, 2016, CNN published an article on their website announcing that the net worth of Bill Gates had then reached $90 billion.[9] For those of us who sit in the cheap seats, that kind of wealth is unimaginable. It won't take long before he will exceed $100 billion since the same article noted that his wealth had increased $6.2 billion in the last year. Bill Gates does not sit alone at the top of that heap. Facebook founder Mark Zuckerberg's wealth increased $8.9 billion and Amazon CEO Jeff Bezos's net worth increased $6.5 billion. All of that in only a year's time.

After I read that article, I said to one of my kids, "Imagine how much good you could do if you had $90 billion at your disposal." We did a little daydreaming.

We could pay for so many needed improvements at the local Bible camp. We would finish our current church building and move in within a few months. How many church missionaries could we support? How many Bibles could we have printed and distributed? How many great, doctrinally sound seminaries could we support? We could train pastors, plant churches, build buildings, support colleges, and fund oversees missions.

Unfortunately, that is not how those immense resources are used. Gates, Soros, Bezos, and many others pour hundreds of millions of dollars each year into supporting the homosexual lobby, abortion on demand, and nearly every other unrighteous cause we can imagine. These contributions not only advance

---

9. http://money.cnn.com/2016/08/23/technology/gates-90-billion/

what the righteous oppose, but they oppose the causes that the righteous would love to see advanced.[10]

In light of his fierce opposition to all things holy, it can seem like a travesty of justice that Bill Gates should even possess that kind of fortune. It appears to be a double travesty that his fortune should increase by $6 billion a year.

Behold, these are the wicked! They are always at ease and they increase in wealth!

---

10. I could not care less that someone has that much wealth. These men have built businesses and provided services that people willingly purchase. I don't begrudge them the fruits of their labors no matter how abundant those fruits might be. So long as they have not used violence or the threat of force to take this money from others, it is theirs. No other person in this world can make a just claim to the fruits of their labors. You will never hear me suggest that these men should pay more in taxes or that the government has a right to their income. I certainly do not believe that the government would make a more righteous use of those resources!

5

A Temptation Avoided

Psalm 73:13–14
Surely in vain I have kept my heart pure
And washed my hands in innocence;
For I have been stricken all day long
And chastened every morning.

Temptations come in many forms. The righteous can be tempted to love the things of this world (1 John 2:15-17), fix their hope on the uncertainty of riches (1 Timothy 6:17), and pursue youthful lusts (2 Timothy 2:22). Temptations to prayerlessness, apathy, greed, worldliness, lust, false doctrine, pride, materialism, sensuality, fear, compromise, and numerous other sins, continually assault the child of God. Such is life in this world under the sun.

We battle sin by putting it to death in the power of the Holy Spirit (Romans 8:13). The Christian life is a continual pursuit of holiness (Hebrews 12:14) in which we "lay aside the old self" and "put on the new self, which in the likeness of God has been created in righteousness and holiness of the truth" (Ephesians

4:23-24). Such a pursuit of holy and righteous living is the mark of those who are led by the Spirit (Romans 8:12-14; Galatians 5:16-26).

There is a unique temptation that threatens to undermine this entire process of sanctification and holy living; it is the temptation to think that holiness and the pursuit of it is of no benefit to a believer. If we start to question the benefit of holy living, we are robbed of our motivation for sanctification. The allure of every other temptation becomes even stronger as our motivation for fighting temptation grows weaker.

Imagine a patient who is afflicted with a half-dozen different terminal diseases. Each of these diseases, if untreated by the appropriate medication, would kill the patient in a matter of months. Appropriately, his doctor has prescribed a combination of medications to treat the diseases. These medications effectively prevent complications from the diseases and enable the patient to live a normal life.

Now imagine that after a couple of years of taking the medications and enjoying the benefits of them, the patient begins to doubt whether the medications are of any benefit to him at all. After all, he sees other men who do not take these medications and they are very healthy. In fact, some of those who do not receive these medications are stronger, faster, and smarter than he. Others who do not take the pills are in far better shape, and enjoy greater health than he has enjoyed in years.

He begins to ask himself if he has not been taking these medications in vain. Every morning he must wake up and diligently take his pills with his breakfast at a prescribed time. Others do not have to endure this inconvenience and they are no worse for wear. Our patient dangerously concludes that his diligence in treating his disease has been of no benefit to him. Such thinking spells certain doom for our afflicted patient.

Seeing the prosperity of the wicked presented a strong and dangerous temptation to Asaph. He was tempted to conclude that living a God-fearing holy life was of no benefit. Asaph was not the first believer to question the benefit of holy living while considering the ease enjoyed by the wicked, and he was certainly not the last.

Given what Asaph has lamented thus far in Psalm 73, his concluding sentiment in verses 13-14 certainly make sense: "Surely in vain I have kept my heart pure and washed my hands in innocence."

Asaph had spelled out in stark detail the difference between the blessings enjoyed by the wicked and the affliction endured by the righteous. From all appearances, he might have concluded that wickedness is rewarded with joy, happiness, and prosperity, while holiness seemed to bring affliction, suffering, and want. Naturally, one would start to wonder if the pursuit of holiness and obedient living was not completely pointless considering this inequity. When the wicked seem to be rewarded and the righteous chastened, they will start to wonder if there is any benefit at all to living a righteous life. The moment such doubts arise in the heart is the very moment one is threatened by a spiritual disaster.

Asaph described his crisis of faith in verse 2: "But as for me, my feet came close to stumbling, my steps had almost slipped." What he describes very generally in verse 2 is expressed quite vividly in verses 13-14. Asaph began to question the value of holiness. He saw the prosperity of the wicked and he was envious of their wealth (v. 3). He began to wonder if a pure heart and a holy life were of any advantage. This would be the most logical conclusion given what he has observed.

Psalm 73:13–14: "Surely in vain I have kept my heart pure and washed my hands in innocence; for I have been stricken all day long and chastened every morning." That is the sound of slipping feet. These are the words of faltering faith.

The Affections of the Godly

Holiness is the natural longing of a redeemed heart. Those whom God has saved have been granted a "repentance that leads to life" (Acts 11:18). They desire to perform "deeds appropriate to repentance" (Acts 26:20) and do not want to live a life that in any way dishonors their Lord. Just as we are commanded to present our bodies as a "living and holy sacrifice, acceptable to God," the true believer desires to be holy and blameless before Him (Romans 12:1; Ephesians 1:4). The true believer wants to be holy because God is holy.

The apostle Peter encouraged his readers with these words:

Therefore, prepare your minds for action, keep sober in spirit, fix your hope completely on the grace to be brought to you at the revelation of Jesus Christ. As obedient children, do not be conformed to the former lusts which were yours in your ignorance, but like the Holy One who called you, be holy yourselves also in all your behavior; because it is written, "You shall be holy, for I am holy." (1 Peter 1:14–16)

The righteous live a life of continual repentance and personal holiness. Asaph was a righteous and God-fearing man and he described his own affections for God and his confidence in his salvation in verses 21-28. He described his own fight against sin in these words:

Psalm 73:13
Surely in vain I have kept my heart pure
And washed my hands in innocence;

There are two elements of personal holiness described in that verse: inward holiness and outward holiness. The "pure heart" refers to inward holiness and "clean hands" describes outward holiness. The struggle against sin must be fought on these two fronts: the heart and the hands. Though these two things are distinct, they are also inseparable.

Asaph was not the only psalmist to recognize the need for clean hands and a pure heart. This language was also used by David in Psalm 24 where he asked, "Who may ascend into the hill of the Lord? And who may stand in His holy place? He who has clean hands and a pure heart, who has not lifted up his soul to falsehood and has not sworn deceitfully" (Psalm 24:3-4). Notice the connection between the soul (inner man) that is lifted up to falsehood and the mouth (outer conduct) that swears deceitfully. Jesus said that "the mouth speaks out of that which fills the heart" (Matthew 12:34). Likewise, Matthew 15:18 says, "But the things that proceed out of the mouth come from the heart, and those defile the man."

Purifying the heart is hard work! We are born in sin and iniquity and spend years of our lives "serving various lusts and pleasures, living in malice and envy, hateful and hating one another" (Titus 3:3-5). Jeremiah 17:9 reminds us that "the heart is more deceitful than all else and is desperately sick; who can understand it?"

The work of the Holy Spirit brings us to a knowledge of our sin (John 16:8-11). What we know of our own hearts at the moment of saving faith is only a glimpse at the true depth of our depravity and wickedness. Though we have been delivered from the penalty of our sin and the power of indwelling sin, we have not yet been delivered from its presence. Sin is still a lingering reality in the life of a believer. We are called to make war against it for the rest of our lives. This can only be done with the assistance of the Holy Spirit who works through the Word of God to sanctify His people in the truth (John 17:17).

The pursuit of holiness is a work in which we cooperate with the Holy Spirit as He works to grow us in holiness. Holiness is something that a believer is to pursue (Hebrews 12:14) and it is something God is working out in our lives. Philippians 2:12–13 beautifully captures these two sides of sanctification: "So then, my beloved, just as you have always obeyed, not as in my presence only, but now much more in my absence, work out your salvation with fear and trembling; for it is God who is at work in you, both to will and to work for His good pleasure." We are commanded to "work out" our salvation even while we recognize that it is God who is at work in us. Paul said a similar thing in 1 Corinthians 15:10–11: "But by the grace of God I am what I am, and His grace toward me did not prove vain; but I labored even more than all of them, yet not I, but the grace of God with me. Whether then it was I or they, so we preach and so you believed." The hard work of pursuing holiness is not a work we do on our own. The grace of God is actively at work in the heart of a believer.

When Asaph says that he "washed his hands in innocence," he is describing outward holiness. Just as Asaph pursued a pure heart, so he avoided sin in order that he may not defile his hands. In today's vernacular, we would say that one has "blood on their hands" if they are guilty of a certain crime. It is a figure of speech to describe their culpability or complicity in some moral wrongdoing. Conversely, hands that are washed in innocence would be those not involved in any impure and defiling activity.

Keeping our hands pure is every bit as difficult as keeping our hearts pure. It requires a vigilance and diligence that is all-consuming. It is more than simply refraining from certain particularly hideous sins that are distasteful to us. It means that we resist temptation, die to ourselves, and deny our flesh. Keeping our hands innocent requires we say no to those sins that are alluring, both big and small. A small lie on our time card, a repeated falsehood, and a lingering look, all defile our hands. This is war for the believer, and it is tough.

Paul encouraged Timothy to "flee from youthful lusts and pursue righteousness, faith, love and peace, with those who call on the Lord from a pure heart" (2 Timothy 2:22). That is a prescription for those who desire clean hands and a pure heart. It is not easy work. Fortunately, God is at work in His people to accomplish His good pleasure. We are empowered by His grace and through His Word to labor toward that end.

All in Vain?

Is it possible that all this work should be in vain? It looked to Asaph as if it had been. He concluded that all this had been done for nothing. "Surely in vain" modifies both statements in the verse. In vain he had kept his heart pure. In vain he had washed his hands in innocence. Both his inward and outward efforts toward purity were called into question.

It is difficult to perceive an advantage in holiness when those who are profane and unbelieving frolic in endless luxury and wealth. If the wicked are rewarded in their sin with ease of life, comfort in death, and increasing wealth, then why pursue righteousness? Spurgeon said one "questions the value of holiness when its wages are paid in the coin of affliction."[1]

Some of the Jews in Malachi's day had started to express the same doubts about serving God. Through Malachi, God confronted the people with their perverse reasoning, even calling such talk "arrogance against Me [the LORD]." Malachi 3:13-15

---

1. Charles Haddon Spurgeon, *The Treasury of David*, Vol. 2, *Psalms 58-110* (Peabody: Hendrickson Publishers), 249.

says, "'Your words have been arrogant against Me,' says the Lord. 'Yet you say, "What have we spoken against You?" You have said, "It is vain to serve God; and what profit is it that we have kept His charge, and that we have walked in mourning before the Lord of hosts? So now we call the arrogant blessed; not only are the doers of wickedness built up but they also test God and escape."'"

Can you hear the cry of Asaph in the words from those of Malachi's day? They called the "arrogant blessed" and observed that those who do wickedly escaped. They openly questioned whether there was any profit in keeping God's law and walking before God in holiness and repentance. Though Asaph faltered far enough to think these thoughts in his mind, he never gave voice to this thinking. He says in verse 15, "If I had said, 'I will speak thus,' behold, I would have betrayed the generation of Your children." Fearing that such thoughts expressed openly would be an act of betrayal toward the children of God, Asaph kept these thoughts to himself. They troubled him (v. 16).

The Afflictions of the Godly

Psalm 73:14
For I have been stricken all day long
And chastened every morning.

There could be no comparison between the wealth enjoyed by the wicked and the affliction appointed for Asaph and other righteous saints. The wicked saw their wealth increase each day (v. 12). The righteous saw their afflictions renewed every morning. The wicked mocked the justice of God and they increased in prosperity. The righteous delighted in God's justice and they were afflicted. The wicked lived without any troubles (v. 5) and the righteous found their troubles persisted every day.

112

When righteous men and women experience trials, tribulations, and suffering, they are not enduring anything out of the ordinary. Contrary to popular evangelical teaching, God has not promised us our best life now. For the righteous, our best life is yet to come. It is the wicked who experience their best life now. The righteous are promised trials, tribulations, temptations, and afflictions.

Paul wrote to his young protégé, Timothy, and told him of the "persecutions, and sufferings, such as happened to [him] at Antioch, at Iconium and at Lystra; what persecutions [he] endured, and out of them all the Lord rescued [him]!" He then warned Timothy, "Indeed, all who desire to live godly in Christ Jesus will be persecuted" (2 Timothy 3:11–12). Suffering and affliction, even at the hands of the ungodly, are something that the obedient Christian should expect. In fact, Paul was so certain he would suffer, that he said to the Thessalonians, "For indeed when we were with you, we kept telling you in advance that we were going to suffer affliction; and so it came to pass, as you know" (1 Thessalonians 3:4).

After preaching the gospel in Lystra on his first missionary journey, Paul was stoned, dragged out of the city, and left for dead (Acts 14:8-18). He was undeterred. After Paul preached the gospel in the city of Derbe, "he returned to Lystra and to Iconium and to Antioch, strengthening the souls of the disciples, encouraging them to continue in the faith, and saying, 'Through many tribulations we must enter the kingdom of God'" (Acts 14:22). The promise of tribulation does not sound like encouragement to our ears. For those undergoing suffering, the encouragement is found in the reassurance that such tribulation accompanies entrance to the kingdom of God.

Jesus' final evening with his disciples (John 13-17) was filled with numerous reminders of coming suffering. He graciously warned the disciples of what was to come, lest in the middle of their sufferings they lose heart and fall away. Jesus said in John 16:33, "These things I have spoken to you, so that in Me you may have peace. In the world you have tribulation, but take courage; I have overcome the world." Earlier Jesus promised them that the world would hate them (John 15:18-25) since it had hated both Him and the Father.

Suffering for righteousness' sake is something that should be embraced. Paul encouraged Timothy in 2 Timothy 1:8, "Therefore do not be ashamed of the testimony of our Lord or of me His prisoner, but join with me in suffering for the gospel according to the power of God."

Finally, let's not forget Peter's encouraging counsel in 1 Peter 4:12–16:

> Beloved, do not be surprised at the fiery ordeal among you, which comes upon you for your testing, as though some strange thing were happening to you; but to the degree that you share the sufferings of Christ, keep on rejoicing, so that also at the revelation of His glory you may rejoice with exultation. If you are reviled for the name of Christ, you are blessed, because the Spirit of glory and of God rests on you. Make sure that none of you suffers as a murderer, or thief, or evildoer, or a troublesome meddler; but if anyone suffers as a Christian, he is not to be ashamed, but is to glorify God in this name.

The modern prosperity gospel is not the biblical gospel. Modern evangelicalism promotes a version of Christianity devoid of sacrifice, suffering, and selflessness. God is portrayed as a cosmic bellhop who exists to meet our needs and shower us with all that our hearts desire. That version of Christianity has no room for suffering and no answers for those who endure the tribulations and afflictions which inevitably come.

Plagues and Troubles

The fact that the righteous suffer and are encouraged to expect afflictions, would do little to comfort Asaph in his crisis of faith. That was the cause of his perplexity. Reminding him that this was not abnormal would do little to sooth his angst. This was precisely Asaph's complaint.

Asaph's mention of his pains and troubles is brief. It is only one verse (v. 14). It is nowhere near the length that he afforded to describing the prosperity of the ungodly (vv. 3-12). That does not mean that Asaph's troubles were not real or even severe. He uses strong and violent words to describe his troubles saying, "For I have been stricken all day long." The word translated "stricken" (NASB, ESV) or "plagued" (NIV, KJV, NKJV) was used to describe making "contact with a limb of the body, or any part of the body, implying, in some contexts, damage to the object touched." It describes being in "a sick or weak condition" and was sometimes used to describe being afflicted with a disease. It is the same graphic word used to speak of the affliction endured by Jesus for the sins of His people in Isaiah 53:4: "Surely our griefs He Himself bore, and our sorrows He carried; yet we ourselves esteemed Him stricken, smitten of God, and afflicted."[2]

The second half of verse 14 is parallel to the first: "And chastened every morning." "Chastened"[3] translates a word that describes "strong disapproval, with possible actions of

---

2. J. Swanson, *Dictionary of Biblical Languages with Semantic Domains : Hebrew (Old Testament)* (electronic ed.). Oak Harbor: Logos Research Systems, Inc., 1997.
3. It is translated "punished" in the NIV and "rebuked" in the ESV.

punishment to follow."[4] The word is used for reproof, rebuke, and correction.

Asaph felt the sting from the rod of God's corrective affliction. If Asaph had committed some grave sin deserving of chastening, he would have offered no complaint. It would not have shaken his faith to the core to face God's correction for grievous sin. Asaph could have expected that. But Asaph was not an impenitent sinner. He was not an ungodly reprobate. He was one who maintained a pure heart and clean hands. He was a godly Jew who walked with God and served Him, yet the troubles he faced were the kind deserved by the wicked described in this psalm. The wicked were due correction, rebuke, and reproof, and yet, they received none. "They are not in trouble as other men, nor are they plagued like mankind" (v. 5).

Not only do the righteous suffer trouble and discipline once, it is continual. We are stricken "all day long" and chastened "every morning." Each new day brings a renewal of the troubles appointed for the righteous. The wicked never face troubles and the righteous are continually bearing them. All day and every day God's people are afflicted with various corrections and trials. Charles Spurgeon wrote, "This was a vivid contrast to the lot of the ungodly. There were crowns for the reprobates and crosses for the elect. Strange that the saints should sigh and the sinners sing. Rest was given to the disturbers, and yet peace was denied to the peace-makers."[5]

It is bad enough to face trials and troubles and bear them continually, but to do this while the wicked strut about facing no similar pains makes this burden nigh unbearable. A godly person can endure a heavy load of trials in this life. It is an added burden

---

4. Swanson.
5. Spurgeon, 250.

to do so while surrounded by the enemies of God who flaunt the ease and luxury of their own existence.

Asaph does not spend a lot of time detailing his own troubles. His complaint is not over the pains of the righteous but the prosperity of the wicked. He is not lamenting the affliction of the godly but the affluence of the ungodly. It does not bother him that the righteous should suffer in this life. It bothers him that the unrighteous do not.

The Temptation

What then is the advantage to being holy? If the pure in heart get troubles and the hard-hearted escape them, if the penitent are afflicted and the impenitent are not, if the righteous are reproved and the wicked are rewarded, why be righteous? What is the incentive to pursue holiness? Why work so hard to keep our hands clean and our hearts pure when it is the unclean and the impure that enjoy all the benefits?

Like Asaph, we would be tempted to conclude that "in vain I have kept my heart pure and in vain I have cleansed my hands." That is a dangerous spiritual state. This is the thinking that led to the spiritual apostasy that Asaph describes in verse 10.[6]

The first half of the psalm begins with a description of Asaph's spiritual peril: "But as for me, my feet came close to stumbling, my steps had almost slipped" (v. 2). It ends on that same note describing the spiritual peril not in terms of his feet but of his mind: "Surely, in vain I have kept my heart pure and wash my hands in innocence."

It is difficult to overstate the precarious nature of such thinking. At no point was Asaph closer to utter spiritual ruin than the moment he began to reason that it was vain to serve God. At

---

6. See the explanation of that passage in the previous chapter.

that moment, his feet were close to stumbling and his steps nearly slipped. Asaph was a man balanced precariously on the edge of the cliff. He was staring into the abyss of utter spiritual ruin and apostasy. The ground beneath his feet was slowly but steadily slipping away. The feeling of despair and utter hopelessness haunted his every thought as he searched for an answer to his question: "Why do the wicked prosper while the righteous suffer?" The more he reflected on the issues the more troublesome they appeared. He might desperately search for some solid truth to clutch, some doctrinal footing that would not give way, but it was to no avail. It appeared that abandoning the truth was the only way to make sense of the injustice that surrounded him.

Left to his own reasoning and limited perspective, Asaph would most certainly slide to spiritual ruin. Thankfully, God does not abandon His people to the peril of apostasy.

Part 2:

The Proper Perspective on the Prosperous

6

The Perspective from the Sanctuary

Psalm 73:15–17
If I had said, "I will speak thus,"
Behold, I would have betrayed
the generation of Your children.
When I pondered to understand this,
It was troublesome in my sight
Until I came into the sanctuary of God;
Then I perceived their end.

One of my favorite animated movies of all time is the cleverly written and much underappreciated movie *Hoodwinked!* featuring the voice talents of Anne Hathaway, Glenn Close, and Patrick Warburton. *Hoodwinked!* is the retelling of "Little Red Riding Hood" featuring several twists. *Hoodwinked!* begins where the traditional tale ends; in grandma's cabin after a scrap between the woodsman and the wolf. Grandma and Little Red Riding Hood feature prominently in the chaos as well.

Stepping in to sort out the mess is a thoughtful, observant inspector who gathers clues by listening to each of the participants tell the story of the previous day from their own perspective. Most of the movie is flashbacks as we relive the events that led up to the chaos in the cabin from the perspective of each of the key figures. As each character relays the events of the day from their unique vantage point, we realize what we thought we knew about the story is not at all the real story. It is not until we have the perspective provided by all four characters that the truth of that day's events becomes clear.

The inspector eventually figures out what is really going on, but not until they all gain a perspective that they did not have at the beginning. For the characters trapped in the details of their own story, they needed a perspective that only someone else could provide.

A Change of Perspective

Psalm 73 reads as if it is two entirely separate psalms. The first half, verses 1-14, recounts a crisis of faith as Asaph struggled to understand why the wicked prosper and the righteous suffer. The second half, verses 15-28, is a jubilant confession of faith after Asaph had gained an eternal perspective on the wicked and the righteous. This eternal perspective is absent in the first half of the psalm.

In the first half of the psalm we get a view of the wicked and their wealth from an earthly perspective. We get the human vantage point from the perspective of time. In the second half of the psalm we get a view of the wicked and their wealth from an eternal perspective. We get to see the arrogant, the boastful, and the proud as God sees them from the perspective of eternity.

When Asaph viewed the wicked and their prosperity from an earthly perspective, it nearly ruined his faith. He could not explain it. He felt compelled to envy the arrogant not for their arrogance but for their affluence. He did not envy their pride but their possessions. He did not desire their wickedness, but their wealth. Once Asaph could see the wicked from God's perspective, he did not envy them. He pitied them.

Asaph's assessment of the wicked in the second half of this psalm is entirely different from that in the first. Suddenly Asaph had a different perspective on their wealth, their security, their relationship to God, their punishment, and the true nature of their material prosperity. Likewise, Asaph had an entirely different perspective on the blessings that the righteous enjoy.

In the first half of the psalm, Asaph spent ten verses (vv. 3-12) describing the wealth and iniquity of the wicked with no mention of their eventual suffering. He spent only two verses (vv. 13-14) describing the suffering of the righteous without providing any description of their blessings. In the second half of the psalm, Asaph spent only three verses on the wicked and their destruction (vv. 18-20) and eight verses (vv. 21-28) describing the glories of God's provision for the righteous both in time and eternity. The first half of the psalm focused almost entirely on the prosperity enjoyed by the wicked, and other than the introductory statement in verse 1, there is no mention of any blessings enjoyed by the righteous. The second half of the psalm is the complete opposite as much is made of the blessings apportioned to the righteous and nothing is said regarding the opulence of the wicked.

In Psalm 73 we see the affluence of the wicked turned to affliction and the agony of the righteous turned to advantage. The prosperity of the wicked becomes their perdition and the travail of the righteous becomes their triumph. Our grief becomes our glory and their riches become their ruin.

To what do we owe this change of perspective? Why was it that Asaph's language, tone, and focus was suddenly changed?

The hinge upon which the entire psalm turns is to be found in verse 17: "Until I came into the sanctuary of God; then I perceived their end." When Asaph came into the place of God's sanctuary, he gained a perspective he previously lacked. He perceived the end of the wicked. Prior to this perspective change, Asaph only evaluated the wicked and their wealth in terms of their current circumstances and not their future judgment.

Asaph's different perspective was not due to a change in his circumstances. He was still "stricken all day long and chastened every morning." The wicked still flaunted their wickedness, set their mouth against the heavens, wore their pride as a necklace, and flaunted their lavish wealth. None of that changed. Asaph was just as bereft of material prosperity in the second half of the psalm as he was in the first. The facts regarding the judgment of the wicked and the blessing of the righteous did not change. The eternal destinies of the wicked and the righteous did not change. God's provision for His own and punishment for His enemies did not change.

What changed? Asaph's perception of the wicked changed. Now he perceived their end, their perdition, and judgment.

A Near Betrayal

Psalm 73:15
If I had said, "I will speak thus,"
Behold, I would have betrayed the
generation of Your children.

Verse 15 will be very confusing unless you remember what we looked at in the last chapter regarding verses 13-14. Asaph had come to the very precarious conclusion that he had served God in vain. He started to think all his efforts toward maintaining clean hands and a pure heart had been rewarded with trials and affliction. Observing the prosperity of those who hated God and the pains of those who loved God, Asaph began to think that loving and serving God was all in vain. He wondered if there was more gain in sinfulness than sanctification.

Though Asaph began to think this way, he never gave voice to this complaint before others. These faithless conclusions may have found a place in his mind but they never found a vent through his mouth. Asaph kept to himself. He realized that if he were to say what he was thinking, it would be an act of betrayal toward the children of God.

We don't know how long Asaph struggled with these issues before they were finally resolved. However long was that season in his life, he weathered it alone, giving no voice to his crisis of faith until it was adequately settled in his own heart and mind. This psalm is the record of that struggle. It was written only after Asaph had come through the clouds of doubt and could boldly declare, "But as for me, the nearness of God is my good." Once Asaph learned the lessons, he shared them with others. Only after Asaph's thinking was righted could the record of his crisis of faith prove to be a benefit and blessing to others.

There is a lesson here for those who have a calling to teach and preach God's word. Teachers and their students are well served when the teacher keeps his personal struggles and doubts to himself until he has adequately worked through those struggles.[1] It is quite in vogue for teachers to share all their struggles, failures, and doubts publicly before those whom they lead. This is done in the name of "openness" and "transparency." I believe this is foolish and has the potential to do great harm to young and weak believers in the congregation. A teacher is given a heavy responsibility: the responsibility to declare the truth

---

1. Pastors/Elders and other teachers in the church should have a group of peers to whom they are accountable and with whom they can share their struggles, trials, and failures. In this way, they can be strengthened by others who will help bear their burden without being a burden to those they teach.

(James 3:1). He is not called to share his struggles with the truth, his doubts about the truth, or his thoughts about the truth. He is called to teach the truth. Any man who is uncertain about the truth has no business teaching it to others.

There is wisdom in Asaph's approach. He said nothing regarding his doubts while he had them. Only after he had learned the valuable lessons recorded in this psalm did Asaph share his struggles with others. He did so in this psalm. By that time, Asaph could help others by sharing those things he had learned during his time of grave temptation and doubt. The struggle that once haunted him could help others, but only after the time of despair had passed and his doubts had been vanquished by a robust faith in the truth.

The word translated "betrayed" means "to be unfaithful, to betray, or to deal treacherously." It can be used to describe acts of unfaithfulness in marriage (adultery) or to God (idolatry).[2] Asaph knew that his feet were near to apostasy once he began to think that it was vain to serve God. To announce this to others would have been a great evil against them.

Asaph knew that God is good to Israel. He knew that God is good to those who are pure in heart (v. 1). Yet he was entertaining a doctrine which was directly contrary to what he knew to be true, namely that God is good to the wicked and afflicts the pure in heart. Asaph recognized these thoughts for the blasphemous poison that they were and refrained from sharing them with others.

Every Christian knows what it is to wrestle with thoughts, doubts, and ideas which we loathe. We have all had moments where some thought popped into our diseased brain that we

---

2. J. Swanson, *Dictionary of Biblical Languages with Semantic Domains : Hebrew (Old Testament)* (electronic ed.). Oak Harbor: Logos Research Systems, Inc., 1997.

instantly hated. Not only did we hate the thought - the idea itself - but we hated ourselves for thinking it, and our brain for giving it a moment's entertainment. Such thoughts make us cry out with the apostle Paul, "Wretched man that I am! Who will set me free from the body of this death?" (Romans 7:24).

Asaph recognized that such doubts about God's goodness, if openly expressed, would do great harm to the people of God. "It is not always wise to speak one's thoughts; if they remain within, they will only injure ourselves; but, once uttered, their mischief may be great. For such a man as the Psalmist, the utterance which his discontent suggested would have been a heavy blow and deep discouragement to the whole brotherhood."[3]

Asaph's unwillingness to publish his doubts, and thus infect others, may have been the means by which God preserved him from utter apostasy. John Calvin notes, "Whilst worldly men give loose reins to their unhallowed speculations, until at length they become hardened, and, divesting themselves of all fear of God, cast away along with it the hope of salvation, he restrains himself that he may not rush into the like destruction."[4] Imagine that Asaph had given voice to his doubts only to find several sympathetic listeners that encouraged his blasphemous conclusions. The more Asaph would share his thoughts, the more reasonable they would sound to himself and to others, until at last he gave up all pursuit of piety and made shipwreck of his faith. It was far better to keep silent regarding his struggles than to do harm to himself and others by spreading what he knew to be a spiritual poison.

---

3. Charles Haddon Spurgeon, *The Treasury of David*, Vol. 2, *Psalms 58-110* (Peabody: Hendrickson Publishers), 250.
4. John Calvin, *Calvin's Commentary on The Book of Psalms,* Vol. 3 (Grand Rapids: Baker Books, 1999), 140.

Though he thought amiss, he took care not to utter that evil thought which he had conceived. Note, it is bad to think ill, but it is worse to speak it, for that is giving the evil thought an imprimatur - a sanction; it is allowing it, giving consent to it, and publishing it for the infection of others....There is nothing that can give more general offence to the generation of God's children than to say that we have cleansed our heart in vain or that it is vain to serve God; for there is nothing more contrary to their universal sentiment and experience nor any thing that grieves them more than to hear God thus reflected on.[5]

Though silence was the right course of action, it only increased Asaph's anguish.

A Painful Silence

Psalm 73:16
When I pondered to understand this,
It was troublesome in my sight

The whole struggle proved to be very painful. Asaph spent time thinking about how the wicked prospered. His mind returned to what he knew: God is good to His own. He critically analyzed the conclusion he had reached: it is vain to serve God. The whole quandary was "troublesome." This was a wearying internal struggle. It was vexing and painful.

Though it would have brought him great relief to be able to share the struggle with others, Asaph knew that would create even more troubles, and those in the hearts of his hearers. He

---

5. Matthew Henry, *Matthew Henry's Commentary on the Whole Bible: Complete and Unabridged in One Volume* (Peabody: Hendrickson, 1994) 848.

was a righteous man and it caused him great grief to struggle with so basic a truth as the goodness of God.

Describing Asaph's dilemma, Spurgeon writes:

> The thought of scandalizing the family of God he could not bear, and yet his inward thoughts seethed and fermented, and caused an intolerable anguish within. To speak might have relieved one sorrow, but, as it would have created another, he forbore so dangerous a remedy; yet this did not remove the first pains, which grew even worse and worse, and threatened utterly to overwhelm him. A smothered grief is hard to endure. The triumph of conscience which compels us to keep the wolf hidden beneath our own garments, does not forbid its gnawing at our vitals. Suppressed fire in the bones rages more fiercely than if it could gain a vent at the mouth. Those who know Asaph's dilemma will pity him as none others can.[6]

The more Asaph thought about this dilemma, and the more he applied human reasoning, the more troublesome the quandary became. He described his anguish in verses 21-22: "When my heart was embittered and I was pierced within, then I was senseless and ignorant; I was like a beast before You."

With the poison of doubt eating away at his soul, Asaph would've longed for a release from his troubling perspective. That release finally came.

The Sanctuary of God

Psalm 73:17
Until I came into the sanctuary of God;
Then I perceived their end.

---

6. Spurgeon, 250.

Something changed. Asaph was in anguish, troubled in soul and spirit until...until he entered the sanctuary of God.

When we read the word "sanctuary," we should not think of that which we typically call a sanctuary in our own day. We associate that word with a particular room where the people of God gather to worship. Asaph is not speaking about a building or a room. The word translated sanctuary simply means "a holy place." The word was used to describe "the sphere of the sacred," that which was set apart for holy use. The troubling thoughts continued until Asaph went into God's holy place.

Where was that? What was that?

It is doubtful that Asaph was describing the temple. He served as a worship leader during the time of David and the temple was not built until after David's death during the reign of Solomon. If Asaph had intended for us to understand him to be speaking of the Tabernacle, the Holy of Holies or some physical location, he would have use language to describe those places. Instead he speaks vaguely of a "sacred place."

I believe it would be an injustice to Asaph's intent if we try to limit this to a particular room or place. It appears that Asaph's intention is much broader than that. I believe he was being intentionally nonspecific. There are many things that Asaph could be referring to, any one of which would have provided him this new perspective.

It's possible that the "sacred place" refers to a place or time of prayer. It might be that Asaph came into God's presence through prayer as he poured out his complaint before God. We know Asaph said nothing about his concerns to the generation of God's children, but we can be certain that Asaph brought his concerns and complaints to his God. It would be in this "sacred place" of prayer with his God, as Asaph poured out his heart before God, that his perspective was changed and he came to perceive the end of the wicked.

It is possible that "sacred place" refers to a place or time of meditation upon God's Holy Word. In meditation, we leave aside those things which are common and profane. In the sanctuary of our mind we focus on those things that pertain to the nature and character of God, His works in this world, and the administrations of His Providence. Contrary to pagan practices of meditation, biblical meditation does not involve emptying our minds, but filling our minds with God's revealed truth - His word. Meditation involves concerted effort to focus our hearts and minds upon revealed truth and the implications of that truth. Meditation is the truth of God percolating in the mind. Perhaps in the context of sacred meditation, Asaph received an entirely new perspective.

Perhaps Asaph is describing his own study of God's Word as a "sacred place." God's revealed word would provide the answers he needed. We can well imagine that Asaph, in this time of tremendous trouble, would give himself to an intense study of God's Word. The reasoning and reflection of his own mind only caused him more trouble (v. 16) and made his heart embittered (v. 21). He would need to turn to an objective revelation to find answers.

Lastly, it is possible that he is describing either private or corporate worship as a "sacred place." It might be that it was during some time set apart for communion, fellowship with the people of God, and worship that Asaph came to understand the true state of the wicked and the true blessings of the righteous.

It is important to note that it is not the particular place that Asaph was concerned with, but a particular perspective. In some way, at some time, through some means, Asaph drew near to God and saw with the eyes of faith what he could not see with eyes of sight. He says in verses 23-24, "Nevertheless I am continually with You; You have taken hold of my right hand. With Your counsel You will guide me, and afterward receive me to glory." When Asaph drew near to God by intentionally coming into the sacred place, God drew near to him and guided him with divine counsel (James 4:8). As a result, Asaph received God's perspective on things which had so long perplexed him.

The sacred place is where God informs our thinking. It is where God's truth instructs our observations. The sacred place is where the Holy Spirit guides our understanding. This is not the place or perspective of human reasoning, profane thinking, or man-centered feelings. It is the place where God is regarded as holy, His Word is the standard by which all things are tested, and human wisdom bows the knee to divine revelation.

The Inadequacy of Human Reason

We should not miss the stark contrast between "ponder to understand" (v. 16) and coming "into the sanctuary of God" (v. 17). It is nothing less than the contrast between human wisdom and divine revelation. Asaph's own pondering troubled and embittered his heart. What Asaph learned in the sanctuary of God liberated his heart.

The human mind - in its fallen state, using natural reason - is incapable of unravelling the mysteries of divine Providence. Despite all his reflection on God's dealings with the wicked and the righteous, Asaph could not comprehend how or why God ordered the affairs of men the way He did. He was unable by his own deliberation and reasoning to understand God's eternal purposes. When the natural man seeks to understand the workings of God by the standard of human reason and wisdom, he must inevitably sink into despair and frustration.

The fallen mind of man is darkened (Ephesians 4:17-19), hostile to God (Romans 8:7-8), and unable to understand spiritual things (1 Corinthians 2:14-16). God is far higher than we and His ways far higher than ours (Isaiah 55:8-9). We are children of dust who seek to know and perceive the hidden purposes of God (Deuteronomy 29:29; Ecclesiastes 3:11-12). The mysteries of Providence and God's sovereign purposes are inaccessible to man unless God should choose to reveal them. It was not his own reasoning that satisfied Asaph and allowed him to perceive the end of the wicked, but entering the sanctuary of God.

As Calvin rightly stated:

> Whoever, therefore, in applying himself to the examination of God's judgments, expects to become acquainted with them by his natural understanding, will be disappointed, and will find that he is engaged in a task at once painful and profitless; and, therefore, it is indispensably necessary to rise higher, and to seek illumination from Heaven.[7]

At another place he says:

> When, therefore, we are here told that men are unfit for contemplating the arrangements of Divine Providence until they obtain wisdom elsewhere than from themselves, how can we attain to wisdom but by submissively receiving what God teaches us by His Word and by His Holy Spirit?[8]

Asaph's change of perspective was due in no part to his own ability to perceive the ways and wisdom of God. It was entirely

---

7. Calvin, 142.
8. Ibid., 143.

due to that holy and humble submission to divine revelation in God's "sacred place."

The End of the Wicked

Asaph's perspective on the wicked was changed when he saw their end. His evaluation of the wicked to this point had been from the perspective of time and not eternity. He had observed how they lived in this life, what they enjoyed in this life, and what they received in this life. When he perceived their end, his attitude toward the wicked changed. God's dealing with the wicked and the righteous seemed eminently unjust until the end of both the righteous and the wicked was factored into the equation.

By "end" Asaph is not referring to their physical death, but their eternal death. He has already described how they die physically and noted that it appears remarkably free from pain and suffering. Verse 4 says, "For there are no pains in their death." Many a wicked man ends his life peacefully facing death because he has convinced himself that his physical death is the end of his existence and conscious being. It is because the wicked believe there is no afterlife that they draw near to death with no pangs of conscience or fear. Contrary to their beliefs, their physical death is not the end of their life, but the beginning of their eternal death under the wrath of God.

By "end" Asaph means their eternal judgment. This is described in the next few verses:

Psalm 73:18–20:
18 Surely You set them in slippery places;
    You cast them down to destruction.
19 How they are destroyed in a moment!
    They are utterly swept away by sudden terrors!

20 Like a dream when one awakes,

O Lord, when aroused,

You will despise their form. [9]

The end of the wicked is contrasted with that of the righteous later in the psalm: "With Your counsel You will guide me, and afterward receive me to glory" (v. 24). The righteous receive eternal glory while the wicked are eternally destroyed.

The nature of the eternal condition of either the wicked or the righteous is not something that can be known from natural revelation or deduced by the human mind. The existence of either Heaven or Hell is not something we can know apart from divine revelation. The glory promised to the righteous and the punishment awaiting the wicked must be revealed to us by God. Otherwise, we could not know it.

If all we knew regarding the wicked came from observing them in this life, we would be forced to conclude that God blesses the wicked with riches and ease. If all we knew regarding the righteous came from observing their experiences in this life, we would be forced to conclude that God punishes and curses the righteous. We too would say, "Surely in vain I have kept my heart pure and washed my hands in innocence" (v. 13). We would know nothing more about the wicked or the righteous. Our understanding of God's goodness would be forever skewed by what we see in this life. Fortunately, we are not left with what we can see in this life only. God has revealed the truth concerning the next.

Evaluating the prosperity of the wicked without considering their end is like evaluating *Gone with the Wind* from nothing but the first two minutes of opening credits. If all we see is the

---

9. We will take a closer look at these verses in the next chapter.

affliction of the righteous without their eternal joy and reward, our perspective on their suffering will be incomplete.

It is foolish and wrong to evaluate the times of the wicked in isolation from their eternity. We can't make sense of their prosperity apart from their certain destruction. In fact, we must evaluate their prosperity in light of their most certain end. When we consider their end, we see that all their prosperity is nothing more than a shiny curse. It is with ease of life they are carried along to certain death, only to be plunged beneath the wrath of God for all eternity when they breathe their last. Their riches blind them to the wrath which is to come.

David Engelsma writes, "In light of the end of the prosperous wicked, all the prosperity of the wicked is seen to be curse, only curse. In light of the end of the troubled saints, all their troubles are blessing, only blessing."[10]

Matthew Henry said:

All is well that ends well, everlastingly well; but nothing well that ends ill, everlastingly ill. The righteous man's afflictions end in peace, and therefore he is happy; the wicked man's enjoyments end in destruction, and therefore he is miserable.[11]

Eternity balances the scales. There is no injustice with God. The end of the story for both the righteous and the wicked has yet to be revealed in full.

---

10. David J. Engelsma, *Prosperous Wicked and Plagued Saints: An Exposition of Psalm 73* (Kindle Locations 612-613). Reformed Free Publishing Association. Kindle Edition.
11. Henry, 849.

7

The Peril of the Wicked

Psalm 73:18–20
Surely You set them in slippery places;
You cast them down to destruction.
How they are destroyed in a moment!
They are utterly swept away by sudden terrors!
Like a dream when one awakes,
O Lord, when aroused,
You will despise their form.

The stark contrast between the lives and eternity of the wicked and the righteous is vividly portrayed in Jesus' account of the rich man and Lazarus[1] in Luke 16. Here are the details as Jesus gave them:

Now there was a rich man, and he habitually dressed in purple and fine linen, joyously living in splendor every day. And a poor man named Lazarus was laid at his gate, covered with sores, and longing to be fed with the crumbs which were falling from the rich man's table;

---

1. This is not the same Lazarus who was a friend of Jesus mentioned in John 11.

besides, even the dogs were coming and licking his sores. Now the poor man died and was carried away by the angels to Abraham's bosom; and the rich man also died and was buried. In Hades he lifted up his eyes, being in torment, and saw Abraham far away and Lazarus in his bosom. And he cried out and said, "Father Abraham, have mercy on me, and send Lazarus so that he may dip the tip of his finger in water and cool off my tongue, for I am in agony in this flame." But Abraham said, "Child, remember that during your life you received your good things, and likewise Lazarus bad things; but now he is being comforted here, and you are in agony. And besides all this, between us and you there is a great chasm fixed, so that those who wish to come over from here to you will not be able, and that none may cross over from there to us." And he said, "Then I beg you, father, that you send him to my father's house - for I have five brothers - in order that he may warn them, so that they will not also come to this place of torment." But Abraham said, "They have Moses and the Prophets; let them hear them." But he said, "No, father Abraham, but if someone goes to them from the dead, they will repent!" But he said to him, "If they do not listen to Moses and the Prophets, they will not be persuaded even if someone rises from the dead."[2] (Luke 16:19–31)

---

2. I am not inclined to the opinion that Jesus is merely telling a parable that is intended to teach a spiritual truth. I hold to the view that this is an actual account of two very real people, one of whom is named Lazarus. If I am correct in this assessment, then the place of torment and the intensity of torment as well as the bliss and joy experienced by righteous Lazarus are all described here. This provides us an account of the afterlife given to us by the One who knows the existence and residence of each of the two men described. If I am wrong and this is only a parable, then this is the only parable Jesus told that names a

This account is strikingly similar to the details of Psalm 73. The rich man lived a life of opulence and splendor. He enjoyed his fine linen and the splendor of abundant provision. The rich man had no mercy upon Lazarus who, in his affliction, ate the crumbs that fell from the rich man's table. The rich man, though it was within his means, did nothing to alleviate the suffering of poor Lazarus. When both men died, their fortunes were entirely reversed. Righteous Lazarus, who spent his life in affliction and suffering, went to his eternal reward. The rich man, who spent his life in wealth and luxury, was in agony. In the story, Abraham described this reversal in verse 25: "Child, remember that during your life you received your good things, and likewise Lazarus bad things; but now he is being comforted here, and you are in agony."

The earthly lives of these two men could not be more different. The eternal state of these two men could not be more different. The earthly life contrasted with the eternal state of each man could not be more different.

We find the same reversal of fortunes in Psalm 73. The wicked, who live their life in opulence and luxury, are cast down to utter and complete destruction in eternal judgment (vv. 18-20). The righteous, who live under the afflictions and chastening of the Lord, are brought to an eternal glory in the presence of a loving God (vv. 23-24). When Asaph finally understood the "end" of the wicked, he saw that their wealth was not something to be

---

main character. Further, if this is not an actual happening and only a parable, we are still justified in believing 1) that Hell is a place of eternal conscious torment that is unbearable, 2) that a place of eternal paradise (Heaven), here referred to as "Abraham's Bosom," exists, 3) that the wicked immediately go to a place of torment at the moment of their death, and 4) that the righteous immediately go to paradise to enjoy the felicity of Heaven. This we believe not based on this passage alone, but on the authority of all that is revealed in Scripture about the afterlife.

envied at all, for it was not the blessing of God upon them, but rather the vehicle of their downfall and judgment. Reflecting upon the end of the wicked also made Asaph more aware of the glorious end promised to the righteous. We will look more at God's provision for the righteous in the next chapter. Here we shall consider the destruction and judgment of the prosperous wicked described in verses 18-20.

Judgment Isn't Pretty

We don't much like to talk about Hell these days. Even in Christian churches, the doctrine is downplayed. I guess we should not be surprised given that the doctrine of sin is avoided like politics at the annual Thanksgiving meal. Skinny-jean-wearing seeker-centered pastors skip past any meaningful talk of sin with terms like "mistakes," "failures," and "bad things." The consequences for sin, including the wrath of a holy God, are rarely proclaimed. Hell is hesitantly mentioned, and only then described as if it weren't one of God's best ideas.

Unlike most seeker-centered churches, the Scripture is unapologetic regarding its teaching about sin, the justice of God, and eternal hell. The descriptions of Hell are graphic, the warnings are strong, and the teachings are clear.

The Old Testament revelation concerning the afterlife is not as detailed and specific as what we find in the New Testament. The Old Testament certainly teaches that there shall be a destruction of the wicked and a glory for the righteous. We see this distinction even in this very psalm that we are studying.

Likewise, details concerning the timing and nature of bodily resurrection are much less clear in the Old Testament than in the New. Job believed that though his skin would be destroyed, his body would be raised (Job 19:23-27). David believed that he would eventually be raised from the dead, and his expression of that belief ended up being a prophetic utterance regarding the resurrection of his greater Son, the Messiah (Psalm 16:10). Bodily resurrection is also described in Isaiah 26:19 and Daniel 12:2. None of this compares to the clear and unambiguous teaching in the New Testament regarding the eternal states of both the wicked and righteous and the nature of resurrected bodies.

Jesus taught that both Heaven and Hell were eternal realities (Matthew 25:46). Hell is described as "fiery Hell" and "eternal fire" (Matthew 5:22; 18:19; 25:41). It is a place of "unquenchable fire" into which bodies are cast (Mark 9:43; Matthew 5:29). In short, Jesus taught that Hell is eternal conscious torment.

The epistles also contain some sobering language regarding the eternal state of the damned. Consider Paul's description in 2 Thessalonians 1:5-10:

> This is a plain indication of God's righteous judgment so that you will be considered worthy of the kingdom of God, for which indeed you are suffering. For after all it is only just for God to repay with **affliction** those who afflict you, and to give relief to you who are afflicted and to us as well when the Lord Jesus will be revealed from heaven with His mighty angels in flaming fire, dealing out **retribution** to those who do not know God and to those who do not obey the gospel of our Lord Jesus. These will pay the **penalty of eternal destruction**, away from the presence of the Lord and from the glory of His power, when He comes to be glorified in His saints on that day, and to be marveled at among all who have believed—for our testimony to you was believed.[3]

Nowhere is Hell mentioned or described as if it is a doctrine of which we should be ashamed. The just damnation of the

---

3. Emphasis mine.

impenitent sinners in eternal conscious torment is an expression of the righteousness, holiness, and justice of God. God is glorified by this doctrine because it magnifies not only His pure and perfect justice, but it also demonstrates the glory of His grace and mercy.

Though all sinners, even for one infraction of God's law (James 2:10), deserve eternal separation from the love and goodness of God, God has condescended to save those who have violated His holy law. He has done this through the work of His Son, the Lord Jesus Christ, by what He did on the cross nearly 2000 years ago.

The divine Son - the second Person of the Trinity - came to this Earth, was born of a virgin, lived a perfect life, then suffered and died a perfect death on the cross, taking the wrath of the Father on behalf of all who will repent of their sin and place their faith in Him. The payment for the sin of all those who seek refuge in the Son was paid in full on Calvary when God poured out His wrath on His Own Son. It was the wrath that we deserve. He took the strokes that we were due (Isaiah 53:3-8).

Jesus Christ did not die for His own sin. He was the "Righteous One" who died in the stead of others as their substitute and their sacrifice (1 Peter 2:24; 2 Corinthians 5:21; John 10:14-18, 25-30). God can now declare us righteous through faith because of what Christ has done (Philippians 2:8-11; Romans 4:5; 5:1-2). Those who are His through repentance and faith have been delivered from the wrath to come.

Any preaching or presentation of the gospel which downplays the gravity of sin and the horror of eternal Hell under the wrath of God diminishes the glory of God in the Gospel.

Hell is a place where eternal justice is meted out. It is where the impenitent are punished for their crimes against a holy, loving, and perfect King. Just as we recoil at the thought that criminals should get away with horrific crimes and escape the justice of the law in this nation, so we should recoil at the thought that the impenitent not be punished in accordance with their crimes. Hell is an eternal punishment because the God Whose law has been violated is an eternal Being, infinite in His perfections and glory. All sin, no matter how insignificant in our eyes, is a high-handed crime against the greatest Sovereign in the universe.

The eternal destruction of the wicked under the holy wrath of God is not a doctrine for which we are to be ashamed. We need not apologize for this truth or for the God who created Hell.[4]

Let's turn now to the description given of the destruction of the prosperous wicked in Psalm 73.

Slippery Footing

Psalm 73:18
Surely You set them in slippery places;
You cast them down to destruction.

Perhaps you have heard someone describe someone else's lot in life with this phrase: "They won life's lottery." That is how we describe those who have affluence and power in our world. If someone was born into wealth, gets a good job, and accumulates a lot of this world's goods, people will say that they "won life's lottery." Even if all they have acquired is the result of their hard work, diligence, and sacrifice, the wealthy are viewed as if the only thing they can credit for their abundance is random chance.

---

4. For more on the subject of Hell, including a defense of the doctrine of eternal damnation, I would recommend *Sinners in the Hands of a Good God: Reconciling Divine Judgment and Mercy* by David Clotfelter and *Hell on Trial: The Case for Eternal Punishment* by Robert A. Peterson.

It was not by chance and happenstance that the prosperous wicked had attained such wealth and power. Their lot in life was not the result of luck. They didn't just "win life's lottery."

Asaph certainly did not believe that the prosperity of the wicked was due to luck. If Asaph had believed that, he would have faced no perplexity over the prosperity of the wicked in life. He would have simply said, "Well, that is how the cookie crumbles. Time and chance overtake us all. It just so happened to work out that way." But Asaph did not respond that way. Because he believed in the sovereignty of God and that nothing can come to any man unless God should give it, Asaph was perplexed. He understood full well that God was the One Who had given to the wicked every last bit of their prosperity. None of what they possessed had come to them by chance - not one dime.

If the wicked enjoyed positions of power, influence, and prestige, it was because God had put them there. It was nothing less than the sovereign hand of God which had brought these men all the trappings of prosperity they enjoyed.

This is what was so disturbing. It seemed as if God were granting prosperity to his enemies as a blessing and withholding such blessing from those who were faithful to Him.

Asaph affirmed that it was the hand of God that exalted these men to their positions of prosperity and notoriety in verse 18: "Surely You set them in slippery places." The "You" in this verse, and those following, is addressed to God. God put these men in this position. God elevated the wicked to their current place. Their current position - as elevated as it appeared – was, in fact, "slippery places," and God had placed them there.

The prosperous vainly believe that their riches are a source of protection and security. Psalm 52:7 pronounces judgment against the man who trusts in his riches: "Behold, the man who would not make God his refuge, but trusted in the abundance of his riches and was strong in his evil desire." The rich view their wealth as a fortress just as the poor view their poverty as their own ruin. Proverbs 10:15 says, "The rich man's wealth is his fortress, the ruin of the poor is their poverty."

As much as they might think their riches provide them safety and security, the proverb warns that it's only in their imagination. Proverbs 18:11: "A rich man's wealth is his strong city, and like a high wall in his own imagination." In the end, their riches do not keep them from the wrath of God. Proverbs 11:4: "Riches do not profit in the day of wrath, but righteousness delivers from death."

They are set in slippery places. The high place to which God has brought them is the very place from which He will cast them down. Verse 18: "You cast them down to destruction." Their position of prosperity and prominence is not a sure, strong, and certain position. It is a slippery place, one from which they can and will quickly fall. This is by the hand of God. God put them in that slippery place, for it was His intention to cast them down from it. The very reason God places the prosperous wicked in their prosperity is so that He might execute their certain doom.

Spurgeon said Asaph "sees that the divine hand purposely placed these men in prosperous and eminent circumstances, not with the intent to bless them but the very reverse....The same hand which led them to their Tarpeian rock[5], hurled them down from it. They were but elevated by the judicial arrangement for

---

5. The Tarpeian Rock (/taːrˈpiːən/) was a steep cliff of the southern summit of the Capitoline Hill, overlooking the Roman Forum in Ancient Rome. It was used during the Roman Republic as an execution site. Murderers, traitors, perjurers, and larcenous slaves, if convicted by the quaestores parricidii, were flung from the cliff to their deaths. Cited by Wikipedia: Samuel Ball Platner, *A Topographical Dictionary of Ancient Rome*, (London: Oxford University Press, 1929) Tarpeius Mons, pp 509-510.

the fuller execution of their doom."[6] John Calvin put it this way: "God for a short period thus lifts them up on high, that when they fall their fall may be the heavier."[7]

We have a proverbial saying in our own day which captures the essence of this: "The bigger they are, the harder they fall." The more powerful, the more influential, the wealthier the wicked become, the more their destruction and sudden loss will pain them. The harder will be their fall from such a position.

God has placed the wicked in the position of prosperity, not to secure them in it, but because it is an insecure and slippery place. He will also most surely cast them down from that position to utter destruction and complete ruin. Yes, God has elevated them. However, His intention is not to bless them by that elevation, but to prepare them for the judgment they so richly deserve. He will most surely bring it to pass.

Moses described the day of God's vengeance upon the wicked: "Vengeance is Mine, and retribution, in due time their foot will slip; for the day of their calamity is near, and the impending things are hastening upon them" (Deuteronomy 32:35).

The Psalms are replete with this kind of language describing the destruction of God's enemies. For instance:

Psalm 37:20:
20 But the wicked will perish;
    And the enemies of the Lord will be like the glory
    of the pastures,
    They vanish - like smoke they vanish away.

---

6. Charles Haddon Spurgeon, *The Treasury of David*, Vol. 2, *Psalms 58-110* (Peabody: Hendrickson Publishers), 251.
7. John Calvin, *Calvin's Commentary on The Book of Psalms*, Vol. 3 (Grand Rapids: Baker Books, 1999), 144.

Psalm 37:35–38:

35 I have seen a wicked, violent man
    Spreading himself like a luxuriant tree in its native soil.
36 Then he passed away, and lo, he was no more;
    I sought for him, but he could not be found.
37 Mark the blameless man, and behold the upright;
    For the man of peace will have a posterity.
38 But transgressors will be altogether destroyed;
    The posterity of the wicked will be cut off.

Psalm 55:23:

23 But You, O God, will bring them down
    to the pit of destruction;
Men of bloodshed and deceit will not live out
    half their days.
    But I will trust in You.

Psalm 92:7:

7 That when the wicked sprouted up like grass
    And all who did iniquity flourished,
It was only that they might be
    destroyed forevermore.

Psalm 94:23:

23 He has brought back their wickedness upon them
    And will destroy them in their evil;
    The Lord our God will destroy them.

The means by which God destroys these particular wicked is their prosperity. Their prosperity and position is the judgment for their wickedness. Asaph erred in that he mistakenly thought that the wicked were getting away with their wickedness. He observed men and women that wore pride like a necklace and violence like garments. The imaginations of their heart were wicked. They mocked God and set their mouth against the heavens. They oppressed the righteous. The wicked presumed that God did not know of their wickedness, and if He did know, He did not care (v. 11).

Not only did God know of their wickedness, He was preparing them for destruction by lavishing them with prosperity. Their wealth was not a blessing, but a curse. The lifting up of the wicked through their prosperity was nothing more than God lifting them up higher that He might crush them upon the rocks of divine judgment harder.

Imagine a medieval executioner commissioned with decapitating a convicted criminal. The stage is set on execution day before an observing crowd. The criminal's head hangs over the edge of the executioner's chopping block; his hands are tightly tied behind his back. The bulky executioner stands above the guilty one, his head covered with a black hood. He grabs his executioner's axe. The edge has been painstakingly sharpened for the occasion and the polished metal glimmers in the sun. The executioner firmly grips the handle and rests the blade on the criminal's neck. Slowly, the executioner begins lifting the axe toward the sky. Higher and higher the axe rises until it is high above the head of the executioner.

Now, imagine, at that very moment, somewhere in the crowd a bewildered observer cries out, "Wait a minute! Don't you know what you are doing? The ax blade is going the wrong way! It is supposed to be moving toward his neck, not away from it!"

So it is with God and the prosperous wicked. He has lifted them up to prosperity and prominence just as an executioner lifts his axe above the neck of the condemned before bringing it down swiftly and precisely. The wicked enjoy their prosperity for only a brief moment just as the condemned enjoys the withdrawal of the blade for a brief moment. In the first half of Psalm 73, Asaph is the bewildered observer who thinks the lifting up of the wicked is a movement in the wrong direction. In verse 18 he came to see that their prosperity was not the blessing of God, it was not a reward for their sin; it was the first stroke of the divine judgment. It was the lifting up of the executioner's axe.

Sound Harsh?

It sounds odd to our modern ear to hear that God judges people through prosperity. That hardly seems like a judgment to us, but that is only because we do not have God's view on prosperity. In our materialistic western culture, we think that prosperity is the goal of life and an evidence of the blessing of God. Most of the Christian church views health and wealth as the central promise of the gospel. Prosperity preachers on "Christian" radio and television teach that abundant riches are the evidence of God's blessing and favor. There is virtually no room in our thinking for the idea that prosperity is not a blessing that God gives to the wicked, but a curse He uses to bring about their destruction.

Prosperity is a curse to the wicked because it hardens their heart. Just as the Lord hardened Pharaoh's heart that He might judge Pharaoh for His own glory and honor,[8] so God hardens the heart of the wicked through their prosperity. Because the wicked are prosperous, they are hardened in their pride and rebellion. Gold becomes their god and their prosperity encourages their idolatry. They are insulated from the affliction and suffering that might turn them to God and draw them near to Him. The trials

---

8. Exodus 7:3, 13, 22; 8:15, 19; 9:7, 12, 35; 10:1, 20, 27; 11:10; 14:4, 8. A few passages describe Pharaoh hardening his own heart: Exodus 8:32; 9:34; 1 Samuel 6:6. One passage describes God hardening the heart of the Egyptians: Exodus 14:17. Deuteronomy 2:30 says God hardened the spirit of Sihon king of Heshbon and made his heart obstinate.

that humble us and teach us not to trust in riches never afflict the prosperous. They are cut off from those graces.

Prosperity encourages the wicked to trust in themselves, their own accomplishments, and their own abilities. Because they live their lives in such comfort and luxury, they cling ever tighter to the things of this world. This only ensures their destruction. At first, they do not want to abandon their creature comforts, eventually they cannot abandon their creature comforts. At first their fortune is their fortress, eventually it becomes their fetters. The prosperity they amass is at first their protection and then their prison.

It may seem harsh to us that God would use riches as a judgment, but that is precisely what this verse teaches. God placed them in their prosperity because riches - worldly affluence - is a "slippery place." God's intention in their prosperity is their judgment and destruction, not their blessing and reward. God is free to judge His creatures in any way that He deems fit. When we consider their end, we see that all their prosperity is nothing more than a shiny curse. Their ease of life carries them along to their certain death only to plunge them beneath the wrath of God for all eternity.

The prosperous wicked are like passengers aboard the Titanic. They're living their lives surrounded by luxury and extravagance, sailing across calm waters, on a still cool evening, with not a care in the world. They think that their prosperity is unsinkable. Their riches create the illusion that they're untouchable and they are deceived by their riches into thinking they will never face a reckoning. Blinded by their luxury, they are completely oblivious to the doom that is about to strike as their "unsinkable fortress" pursues a crash course with a judgment destined to end their lives of ease in an instant. Their riches blind them to wrath that is to come.

But What about the Prosperous Righteous?

We should not conclude from these verses that God *always* gives prosperity as a judgment nor that prosperity is *always* a judgment.

God does not *always* judge the wicked through prosperity. There are plenty of wicked people who live in poverty. The fact that they do not enjoy prosperity does not make them any less wicked, nor any less deserving of divine judgment. The lazy lout who spends his days blaspheming, drinking, and carousing, then comes home to his double-wide and beats his wife and children before falling to sleep in a drunken stupor may live a meager life in terms of this world's wealth, but he is no more righteous than the prosperous wicked described in Psalm 73. Such a person has earned God's judgment, and the Lord most certainly will avenge that evil, but it is obviously not going to be through prosperity. God does not always judge the wicked through prosperity.

Likewise, prosperity is not always a judgment. Scripture is filled with men who enjoyed the grace of riches as a gift from the hand of God. Abraham, Isaac, Jacob, Joseph, Job, David, and Noah, are all examples of men to whom God gave tremendous wealth. Just as God is free to use prosperity as a curse and judgment upon the wicked, so he is free to use prosperity as a blessing and grace given to the righteous. Prosperity is not promised in the gospel. That does not mean that the Lord does not put a good deal of this world's riches into the hands of those who please Him. Proverbs 10:22: "It is the blessing of the Lord that makes rich, and He adds no sorrow to it." In the case of the wicked, God adds to their prosperity the sorrow of their eternal judgment.

The Lord is free to execute his judgments through whatever means He deems best. If wealth and riches can be used by God to curse the wicked and increase their judgment, He is free to do so. We may not view prosperity as a judgment, but that is because we do not see what God is accomplishing through the prosperity He grants to the wicked. The problem is not with the means which God has chosen, but with our ability to understand the way He works through those means.

From Envy to Pity

In light of what we learn from this verse, why would we ever envy the wealth of the wicked? Who in their right mind would envy the means of someone's judgment? Who would wish to have as their own the downfall and destruction that awaits these impenitent rebels? Certainly we would never wish we were the convicted criminal with his neck upon the block awaiting the plunge of the executioner's axe. Would you wish to be under the executioner simply because the axe is on its way up?

God forbid! Rather, "we ought to be of God's mind, for His judgment is according to truth, and not to admire and envy that which He despises and will despise; for, sooner or later, He will bring all the world to be of His mind."[9]

The downfall and destruction of the wicked is certain. This is evident in the fact that God has placed them in a slippery place so that in due time, their feet may stumble. Their fall will be great.

At this realization, our envy should turn to pity. The righteous do not gloat over the death or downfall of the wicked. Their destruction, their suffering, their eternal damnation is not a source of joy for those who know Christ and the gracious forgiveness that He has provided.

God will most certainly delight in the execution of His judgment as He avenges Himself on His enemies. God does not

---

9. Matthew Henry, *Matthew Henry's Commentary on the Whole Bible: Complete and Unabridged in One Volume* (Peabody: Hendrickson. 1994) 849.

judge sin reluctantly. He judges sin so that justice and righteousness may be vindicated. Psalm 33:5 says, "He loves righteousness and justice; The earth is full of the lovingkindness of the Lord."[10] Such judgment is no violation of His love, grace, or compassion.

It is appropriate for the righteous to rejoice when God's name is vindicated, justice is done, and the sin of the wicked is punished by God. Proverbs 21:15 says, "The exercise of justice is joy for the righteous, but is terror to the workers of iniquity." Proverbs 11:10 describes the rejoicing of the righteous over the downfall of the wicked: "When it goes well with the righteous, the city rejoices, and when the wicked perish, there is joyful shouting." Psalm 107 describes the judgment of God upon the rebellious and His deliverance of His people. Near the end of the psalm, we read, "The upright see it and are glad; but all unrighteousness shuts its mouth" (Psalm 107:42). The righteous are glad over the deliverance of God's people and the judgment of God's enemies. Psalm 58:10: "The righteous will rejoice when he sees the vengeance; He will wash his feet in the blood of the wicked."

The nations are encouraged to rejoice at the execution of God's justice. Deuteronomy 32:43: "Rejoice, O nations, with His people; for He will avenge the blood of His servants, and will render vengeance on His adversaries, and will atone for His land and His people." Moses rejoiced at the destruction of Egypt along with Pharaoh's army and the deliverance of God's people from their oppressors (Exodus 15).

---

10. See also Psalm 89:14: "Righteousness and justice are the foundation of Your throne; lovingkindness and truth go before You," and Psalm 97:2: "Clouds and thick darkness surround Him; righteousness and justice are the foundation of His throne."

Likewise, the book of Revelation features scenes of rejoicing in Heaven among the saints and angels over the justice of God in the destruction of the impenitent wicked on earth. At the destruction of Babylon, Revelation 18:20 says, "Rejoice over her, O heaven, and you saints and apostles and prophets, because God has pronounced judgment for you against her."

Look at the scene of hallelujahs and worship over the judgment of the wicked in Revelation 19:1–4:

> After these things I heard something like a loud voice of a great multitude in heaven, saying, "Hallelujah! Salvation and glory and power belong to our God; because His judgments are true and righteous; for He has judged the great harlot who was corrupting the earth with her immorality, and He has avenged the blood of His bond-servants on her." And a second time they said, "Hallelujah! Her smoke rises up forever and ever." And the twenty-four elders and the four living creatures fell down and worshiped God who sits on the throne saying, "Amen. Hallelujah!"

All of Heaven sings the song of the Lamb. Revelation 15:3 says, "And they sang the song of Moses, the bond-servant of God, and the song of the Lamb, saying, 'Great and marvelous are Your works, O Lord God, the Almighty; righteous and true are Your ways, King of the nations!'" Truly God's judgments are righteous. His ways are true. His justice is holy and right. The redeemed say so.

It would be improper to rejoice if sin were overlooked, if blasphemies against God and wickedness done against His kingdom and His people were not punished justly and appropriately. We should be surprised if we were not expected to rejoice at the display of God's justice. Since justice is the foundation of God's throne and an essential element of His nature, it is unthinkable that the righteous would not rejoice when God displays that aspect of His nature. How can Christians long for the Kingdom of Christ and pray for that Kingdom to come if they do not rejoice in the justice that will accompany the full manifestation of that Kingdom?

Obviously there is an extreme that should be avoided. We do not delight in the justice of God because we wish ill upon individual people and delight in their death, their pain, or their suffering. It is the righteous judgments of God which are our delight, not the sufferings of our fellow man. We should feel pity for those who are the objects of God's just wrath while rejoicing in the glory of God manifested in that wrath against sin. It is not impossible to be both thankful for God's justice and sorrowful over the lost condition of those who face it.

Sudden Destruction

Psalm 73:19
How they are destroyed in a moment!
They are utterly swept away by sudden terrors!

Their destruction comes suddenly. It takes but a moment for their fall. In a flash, in the twinkling of an eye, the prosperous wicked fall from their slippery place into sudden terrors. Asaph is describing a sudden and swift destruction. There is a sense of wonder over it. "How they are destroyed in a moment!" That is an expression of godly astonishment over the suddenness of this destruction.

When Asaph describes their destruction as sudden, he is not saying it will be immediate. Though they are "destroyed in a moment" the timing of that destruction may be a long way off from our earthly perspective. Let's return to the earlier illustration of the condemned criminal and the executioner. Though the stroke of the executioner's axe will only take a moment to end the life of the condemned, that execution may be delayed for an extended time. For instance, the judge may, upon pronouncement of sentence, schedule the execution for one year from the day the verdict is read. The criminal's execution is not immediate, but when it comes, it happens in a moment.

Spurgeon said:

> Headlong is their fall; without warning, without escape, without hope of future restoration! Despite their golden chains, and goodly apparel, death stays not for manners but hurries them away; and stern justice unbribed by their wealth hurls them into destruction....The momentary glory of the graceless is in a moment effaced, their loftiness is in an instant consumed.[11]

Their wealth and prosperity can buy them everything in this life, and nothing in the next. They cannot bribe the God of eternal justice. The glory, wealth, prosperity, power, and influence which they think is so lasting and so enduring, is in a moment eclipsed. It is gone. Earlier, Asaph described the death of the wicked as being without pains. "For there are no pains in their death" (Psalm 73:4).

That may in fact be true. They may end this life pain-free, but they do not begin eternity that way. Though they may die in comfort, they'll wake in everlasting pains. This change happens suddenly, in a moment. In an instant, the impenitent prosperous wicked move from luxury to destruction. In a moment, the wicked lose everything. He is plunged from his pedestal - his slippery place - into the abyss of eternal ruin. At that moment,

---

11. Spurgeon, 251.

the wicked will realize that all their prosperity, ease, and comforts only served to ripen them for this ruin.

The destruction of the wicked is described as "sudden terrors." They are suddenly swept away into the wrath of God to face unimaginable terrors for eternity. "It is a terrifying thing to fall into the hands of the living God" (Hebrews 10:31) because "our God is a consuming fire" (Hebrews 12:29).

The final judgment of the wicked is described in Revelation 20:11–15:

> Then I saw a great white throne and Him who sat upon it, from whose presence earth and heaven fled away, and no place was found for them. And I saw the dead, the great and the small, standing before the throne, and books were opened; and another book was opened, which is the book of life; and the dead were judged from the things which were written in the books, according to their deeds. And the sea gave up the dead which were in it, and death and Hades gave up the dead which were in them; and they were judged, every one of them according to their deeds. Then death and Hades were thrown into the lake of fire. This is the second death, the lake of fire. And if anyone's name was not found written in the book of life, he was thrown into the lake of fire.

The prosperous wicked cannot avoid the day when they shall face the just wrath of God for their sin. They will find that all their acts of oppression, violence, and blasphemy (vv. 3-10), were not forgotten (v. 11). They will realize that while they thought they were escaping the judgment of God, they were in fact storing up wrath for themselves - a wrath that reveals the righteous judgment of God. On that day, "There will be tribulation and distress for every soul of man who does evil, of the Jew first and also of the Greek, but glory and honor and peace to everyone who does good, to the Jew first and also to the Greek" (Romans 2:9-10).

They will be swept away in terror as they face the justice of Him from Whose presence earth and Heaven flees.

Certain Judgment

Psalm 73:20
Like a dream when one awakes,
O Lord, when aroused,
You will despise their form.

The prosperous life of the wicked is compared to a dream from which they will eventually awake. Their life of wealth and ease is no more substantial than the images of a dream. Like a dream, it will pass quickly, and once awakened, they will realize it was little more than a mirage.

Perhaps you have had dreams in which you had something, or several things, that you have always wanted. In your dream, you felt so secure, satisfied, and joyful. How disappointed you were when you woke up and realized it was only a dream! The riches you enjoyed are no more. What you possessed in the dream has no bearing upon your lot in reality. The luxury, joy, and delights of your dream vanish the instant you awake.

So it is with the prosperity of the wicked. Their wealth in this life is nothing more than a temporary, transitory, vapor. When this life is over and judgment has come, they will look back upon their wealth the way we view a dream. How quickly it came! How quickly it is gone! How sobering is their reality! Matthew Henry notes:

What their prosperity now is; it is but an image, a vain show, a fashion of the world that passes away; it is not real, but imaginary, and it is only a corrupt imagination that makes it a happiness; it is not substance, but a mere shadow; it is not what it seems to be, nor will it prove what we promise ourselves from it; it is as a dream, which may please us a little, while we are asleep, yet even then it disturbs our repose; but, how pleasing soever it is, it is all but a cheat, all false; when we awake we find it so. A hungry man dreams that he eats, but he awakes and his soul is empty (Isa. 29:8). A man is never the more rich or honourable for dreaming he is so. Who therefore will envy a man the pleasure of a dream?[12]

For the time being, they enjoy their dream only by the forbearance of God which forbearance is likened to sleep. Delay in God's action against sinners appears from our vantage point as if God were asleep. God being aroused from that sleep is a figurative way of describing the sudden way in which God will take action to judge the wicked. This poetic language is used elsewhere as well. In Psalm 44:23 we read, "Arouse Yourself, why do You sleep, O Lord? Awake, do not reject us forever." Psalm 35:23 calls upon God to "stir up Yourself, and awake to my right and to my cause, my God and my Lord."

Psalm 59:4–5:
4 For no guilt of mine, they run and set themselves
    against me.
    Arouse Yourself to help me, and see!
5 You, O Lord God of hosts, the God of Israel,
    Awake to punish all the nations;

---

12. Henry, 849.

Do not be gracious to any who are treacherous
    in iniquity. Selah.

The language regarding God sleeping is only poetic imagery used to describe the delay in the execution of God's judgment on the wicked and His deliverance of the righteous. Psalm 121:4 reminds us, "Behold, He who keeps Israel will neither slumber nor sleep."

Like the prosperity of the wicked, the inactivity of God is only an illusion. We have learned from the psalm that God is actively judging the wicked through their prosperity. God is at work hardening their hearts, blinding their eyes, and ripening rebels for His justice. He is not ignorant of their sin (v. 11). He is not sleeping through their prosperity, but actively using it to prepare them for judgment.

Modern translations vary a little in their rendering of the last phrase of the verse. The difference has to do with the meaning of "form."

KJV: Thou shalt despise their image.

NKJV: You shall despise their image.

NASB: You will despise their form.

NIV: You will despise them as fantasies.

ESV: You despise them as phantoms.

The word "despise" has the basic meaning "to accord little worth to something."[13] According to the Theological Wordbook of the Old Testament, "While this action may or may not include overt feelings of contempt or scorn, the biblical usage indicates that the very act of undervaluing something or someone implies contempt."[14]

There are three possible interpretations for the verse.

First, "form" refers to the wicked themselves. It is their image, the representation of themselves, which the Lord despises.[15] This would mean that God does not value them, but rather views them as something of little worth. This stands in stark contrast with the worth that the wicked would attribute to

---

13. R.L. Harris, G.L. Archer Jr., & B.K. Waltke,(Eds.). (1999). *Theological Wordbook of the Old Testament* (electronic ed., p. 98). Chicago: Moody Press.
14. Ibid.
15. Some are very uncomfortable with the idea that God should have anything but overwhelming love for the wicked. They have no room in their thinking for the notion that God's affections should include a form of hatred for those who work iniquity. They would say that "God hates the sin but loves the sinner." I do not deny that God has a love for the sinner since the sinner is still a creature made in His image. The love that God has for the sinner is not a redeeming love that moves to rescue him in the way that He loves and rescues the bride of Christ (Ephesians 5:25-30). The love that Christ has for His sheep is a redeeming love that saves His sheep everlastingly (John 10:11-18, 25-30). God does not love all people the same way, nor to the same end. Just as it is not fit to deny that God has a certain love for the wicked, neither is it right to deny that Scripture reveals that God has a hatred for the wicked as well. Psalm 5:5 says, "The boastful shall not stand before Your eyes; You hate all who do iniquity." Hosea 9:15 says, "All their evil is at Gilgal; indeed, I came to hate them there! Because of the wickedness of their deeds I will drive them out of My house! I will love them no more; all their princes are rebels." See also Leviticus 20:23. Proverbs 6:16-19 says, "There are six things which the Lord hates, yes, seven which are an abomination to Him: haughty eyes, a lying tongue, and hands that shed innocent blood, a heart that devises wicked plans, feet that run rapidly to evil, a false witness who utters lies, and one who spreads strife among brothers." It may be difficult for us to understand how these two affections, love and hatred toward the wicked, can exist simultaneously in God. That difficulty should not drive us to deny what Scripture teaches concerning this reality.

themselves. They strut about in pride and arrogance (v. 6) setting their mouth against Heaven (v. 8). Adorned with chains of gold, the prosperous wicked highly value themselves. God does not share that estimation. In God's eyes, their wealth adds to them no value. God sees them for what they are in truth: children of dust, rebellious enemies deserving of His wrath.

Second, "form" refers to the idols of the wicked. The word is used sixteen times and to quote the *Theological Wordbook of the Old Testament* again:

> The word basically refers to a representation, a likeness. Five times it is used of man as created in the image of God. Twice it is used of the golden copies of the mice and swellings that afflicted the Philistines (I Sam 6:5, 11). Mostly it refers to an idol."[16]

If this is the sense in which Asaph is using the word, then it likely refers to the wealth and prosperity which the wicked idolize. Their wealth is the idol in which they trust, the god that they serve. In judgment, God shows His contempt for their "idol." God certainly does not value prosperity, riches, and affluence the way the wicked do. He looks down upon it is a useless and worthless thing.

Third, "form" refers to their "dream" mentioned at the beginning of the verse. In keeping with this understanding, the NIV translates the word as "fantasies." The ESV follows suit and uses the word "phantoms."

This third interpretation seems to fit best with the immediate context, especially the phrase at the beginning of the verse. Asaph compares the prosperity of the wicked, the life they live, and the ease they enjoy to the brevity and worthlessness of a dream. All their luxury is worth no more than a fantasy. It is only

---

16. Harris, Archer, Waltke, 767.

a phantom. Thus, God despises it. He looks down upon it as a worthless thing. God's evaluation of their prosperity and ease of life is the true and accurate assessment of these luxuries.

When God's justice awakes, the sinner will find that the riches they enjoyed were momentary but the misery they will endure is everlasting.

The greater the comforts and prosperity of the wicked in this life, the greater will be their loss when they step into the next. The greater the suffering and affliction of the righteous in this life, the greater will be their gain the moment they enter the next.

The challenge for us is clear: will we envy these things as if they have real value? or will we pity those who face God's wrath when their brief dream is over?

8

The Provision for the Righteous

Psalm 73:21-28
When my heart was embittered
And I was pierced within,
Then I was senseless and ignorant;
I was like a beast before You.
Nevertheless I am continually with You;
You have taken hold of my right hand.
With Your counsel You will guide me,
And afterward receive me to glory.
Whom have I in heaven but You?
And besides You, I desire nothing on earth.
My flesh and my heart may fail,
But God is the strength of my heart
and my portion forever.
For, behold, those who are far from You will perish;
You have destroyed all those who
are unfaithful to You.
But as for me, the nearness of God is my good;
I have made the Lord God my refuge,
That I may tell of all Your works.

What a change has come in the second half of this psalm! Asaph has moved from envying the wicked to pitying them. He has seen that since the afflictions of the righteous end in peace, we are truly happy and blessed, for we are forever happy and blessed. Further, the prosperity of the wicked ends in destruction and misery; therefore, they are truly miserable, for they are eternally miserable.

Would you envy the ox that is being fattened for the slaughter? You may observe his easy life, the comforts of his stall, and his constant provision. The ox eats his fill of the finest grain every day. He lays around his pen while others work to provide his food and clean up his mess. Continually relaxing, he lives with never a worry in the world. Do you envy him? Knowing the end of the ox, he should be the object of your pity and not your envy. We ought never to envy that which God despises.

An eternal perspective reveals to us that the wicked are not the objects of God's blessing, the righteous are. We have been delivered from the wrath of God. We have been delivered from eternal destruction. God is good to His people, for He has rescued them from the "slippery place" of the wicked. The righteous are not cast down in a moment to destruction. Death does not bring the beginning of eternal misery for those who belong to God through faith in Christ, but eternal joy and pleasures forevermore (Psalm 16:11).

An eternal perspective also reveals that the righteous are not cursed by God in this life. The afflictions of this life bring us to eternal glory. The chastening of this life is for those whom God loves (Hebrews 12:4-11). It is the wicked who are cursed by God through the wealth that He uses to blind them and eventually destroy them.

That God gives these earthly treasures to His enemies should tell us something of the true value of riches. If financial prosperity were truly the blessing that we often think, God would not give so much of it to those who have the least of His love. God has reserved those things which are of worth for His elect. Romans 8:32: "He who did not spare His own Son, but delivered Him over for us all, how will He not also with Him freely give us all things?" The fact that prosperity is given to the wicked by the hand of God speaks volumes about the nature of these riches. Their value is only for this life. Those things which are of eternal worth, infinite and lasting value, are reserved for those who are His. God is good to those who are pure in heart. He gives to His elect everything of value. He gives prosperity to the rest.

The Temporal Versus the Eternal

The rest of this Psalm - verses 21-28 - focuses on the blessings and benefits that accrue to the righteous.

The first half of this psalm spent ten verses describing the prosperity of the wicked from an earthly perspective (vv. 3-10). Very little is said about the righteous. Only two verses speak of the righteous. Those two verses are negative in tone, questioning the advantage of righteous living. We have seen that the second half of this psalm is very different. There are only three verses about the wicked, and they describe their destruction. By contrast, there are eight verses that describe the blessings of the righteous. Verse 27 does speak of those who will perish, but even that is intended to emphasize the blessings given to the righteous.

Asaph does not offer us a comprehensive list of the blessings promised to the righteous. That is not his intent. Instead, he describes those blessings which are of eternal significance. Asaph is contrasting the fleeting nature of prosperity with the eternal nature of the blessings the righteous enjoy. The first half of the psalm contrasts the righteous and the wicked in this life. The second half contrasts the righteous and the wicked in the next. Verses 21-28 focus on the end - eternal joy - of the righteous.

We can examine these numerous grand benefits under three headings: the grace of God in forgiveness (vv. 21-22), the guidance of God to glory (vv. 23-24), and the goodness of God for eternity (vv. 25-28).

Grace of God in Forgiveness

Psalm 73:21–22
When my heart was embittered
And I was pierced within,
Then I was senseless and ignorant;
I was like a beast before You.

These are words of contrition and confession. Asaph is describing the time he spent in his sinful thinking regarding the wicked. Asaph's sin is described in verse 3: "For I was envious of the arrogant as I saw the prosperity of the wicked." He looked upon the riches of the wicked and he envied their possessions. He wished he could enjoy those riches, for he mistakenly assumed them to be tokens of God's blessing. As we have seen, this perspective was entirely wrong. His envy was sinful.

Asaph described the blasphemous conclusion he had reached in verses 13-14: "Surely in vain I have kept my heart pure and washed my hands in innocence; for I have been stricken all day long and chastened every morning." Asaph found himself entertaining in his mind falsehoods regarding God's nature, His blessings, and His goodness.

This stinking thinking caused Asaph tremendous spiritual and emotional suffering. He was embittered and pierced in his innermost being. Such thinking may seem reasonable and rational to an unbeliever - one whose heart has not been renewed by grace - but it could not be entertained in the heart of a believer without serious spiritual angst.

The word translated "embittered" means "to be fermented, sour, or leavened."[1] It is used here figuratively to describe Asaph's negative attitude. Though Asaph does not reveal the object of his bitterness and sour attitude, we can surmise some possibilities.

Envying the prosperity of the wicked can make one bitter against God. Asaph wrongly assumed their prosperity to be a token of God's blessing. This soured his affections toward God. Why would God bless the wicked? Why would God pour out such rewards upon those who dishonor Him? Why would He withhold such blessings from those who are His chosen ones? Asaph wondered why God would not only keep such blessings from him, but give them to those who are entirely unworthy of them. This was surely a source of bitterness.

Envying the prosperity of the wicked can make one bitter against the wicked. We typically grow bitter against those we envy. We covet their possessions and what we perceive as their "blessings." The more we fixate on the things we don't have but wish we did, the more we grow embittered and sour against those who have them.

An embittered heart has the potential to defile not only our own soul but many others as well. The author of Hebrews warned, "See to it that no one comes short of the grace of God; that no root of bitterness springing up causes trouble, and by it many be defiled" (Hebrews 12:15–16).

Asaph's sinful thinking caused him pain deep in his soul. He was "pierced within." Sinful thoughts in the mind of a good man are painful and grievous to him. Sinful thinking sours the inner

---

1. R. L. Harris, G. L. Archer Jr., &, B. K. Waltke (Eds.), *Theological Wordbook of the Old Testament* (electronic ed., p. 297). Chicago: Moody Press.

man. Spurgeon said, "We see how bitterly good men bewail mental wanderings; they make no excuses for themselves, but set their sins in the pillory, and cast the vilest reproaches upon them. O for grace to detest the very appearance of evil!"[2]

Asaph openly confessed that his sinful thinking was both ignorant and senseless. This is the confession of a man who is truly contrite over his sin. From the vantage point of the sanctuary, Asaph saw the vanity and foolishness of his earlier thoughts. He likened it to the reasoning of a mere animal.

Animals give no thought to the future and evaluate their circumstances in light of the present only. They are aware of only those realities communicated to them through their five senses. They judge all their happiness, contentment, and satisfaction upon outward appearances and immediate experiences. So had Asaph. He had looked upon the prosperity of the wicked and observed their sin. He saw how they lived and how they died. His entire evaluation of the wicked and their prosperity had been no more perceptive than that of a brute beast. Just as an animal might judge everything by the sight of the eyes, so Asaph had judged everything merely by appearances.

Matthew Henry summarized Asaph's statement this way:

Beasts mind present things only, and never look before at what is to come; and so did I. If I had not been a great fool, I should never have suffered such a senseless temptation to prevail over me so far. What! to envy wicked men upon account of their prosperity! To be

---

2. Charles Haddon Spurgeon, *The Treasury of David*, Vol. 2, *Psalms 58-110* (Peabody: Hendrickson Publishers), 252.

170

ready to wish myself one of them, and to think of changing conditions with them! So foolish was I.[3]

Psalm 92:6–7:

6 A senseless man has no knowledge,
     Nor does a stupid man understand this:
7 That when the wicked sprouted up like grass
     And all who did iniquity flourished,
It was only that they might be
     destroyed forevermore.

That perfectly describes the sinful thinking of Asaph in the first half of Psalm 73. He lacked the understanding that the flourishing of the wicked was only temporary and resulted in their everlasting destruction. In the words of Psalm 92, it is the "senseless man" and "stupid man" who does not understand this.

By the grace of God, Asaph was rescued from his foolish thinking, sour heart, and spiritual anguish. God allowed him to see the end of the wicked and the end of the righteous. In His grace, God granted repentance to Asaph.[4] Asaph found forgiveness for the sin he confessed. He had every confidence that God would receive him to glory (v. 24).

The Guidance of God to Glory

Psalm 73:23–24
Nevertheless I am continually with You;
You have taken hold of my right hand.

---

3. Matthew Henry, *Matthew Henry's Commentary on the Whole Bible: Complete and Unabridged in One Volume* (Peabody: Hendrickson 1994) 849.
4. Scripture teaches that repentance is a gift that God grants to His people. See Acts 5:31; 11:18; and 2 Timothy 2:25. This does not in any way negate the positive command to sinners to repent of sin and turn to God. See Acts 17:31; 1 Thessalonians 1:9-10.

With Your counsel You will guide me,
And afterward receive me to glory.

Asaph had keenly felt his spiritual danger. He knew that his feet were "close to stumbling." He had "almost slipped." Once rescued from his embittered heart and spiritual anguish, he credited God with his spiritual preservation. In spite of his sinful and brutish thinking, Asaph was kept from spiritual apostasy by nothing less than the preserving grace of God. Though his feet came close to slipping, they never fully slipped. Though he looked into the abyss of apostasy, the Lord preserved him from falling headlong to utter spiritual ruin. This is the keeping work of a God Who saves fully all who trust in Him.

He was confident of God's presence. Even while in his spiritual angst, with his feet near to apostasy, God's presence abided with him still. Asaph may not have felt God's presence in the midst of his spiritual trouble. He may have felt embittered and estranged from the very God he worshiped and served. God's presence was with him still. God does not abandon His people to spiritual ruin. He never will (Hebrews 13:5). Asaph did not have himself to credit for God's presence. It was God who took hold of Asaph, not the other way around. "You have taken hold of my right hand." It is only on this side of his spiritual crisis that Asaph realized the presence of God and knew the goodness of that presence.

Calvin wonderfully described this keeping presence of God by distinguishing between our perception of His presence and the reality of that presence even when we are ignorant of it. He writes:

Men are said to be with God in two ways; either, first, in respect of apprehension and thought, when they are persuaded that they live in His presence, are governed

172

by His hand, and sustained by His power; or, secondly, when God, unperceived by them, puts upon them a bridle, by which, when they go astray, He secretly restrains them, and prevents them from totally apostatising from Him. When a man therefore imagines that God exercises no care about him, he is not with God, as to his own feelings or apprehension; but still that man, if he is not forsaken, abides with God, inasmuch as God's secret or hidden grace continues with him. In short, God is always near His chosen ones; for although they sometimes turned their backs upon Him, He nevertheless has always His fatherly eye turned towards them.[5]

Asaph was thankful for the restraining and sustaining presence of God that kept him from falling forth into apostasy and open blasphemies. He knew God had taken him by his right hand.

The imagery of God taking His child by the hand is a comforting one. Those who have God at their right hand are said to be secure. Psalm 16:8: "I have set the Lord continually before me; Because He is at my right hand, I will not be shaken."

Contrast God's gracious grip on the hand of the righteous with his judgment on the arms of the wicked in Psalm 37:17: "For the arms of the wicked will be broken, but the Lord sustains the righteous."

Though the righteous will certainly stumble and fall, God has secured them in the grip of His loving hand. Psalm 37:24 says, "When he falls, he will not be hurled headlong, because the Lord

---

5. John Calvin, *Calvin's Commentary on The Book of Psalms,* Vol. 3 (Grand Rapids: Baker Books, 1999), 151-152.

is the One who holds his hand." Psalm 63:8 says, "My soul clings to You; Your right hand upholds me."

The same promise was intended to be an encouragement to the nation of Israel in Isaiah 41:10 and 13:

> 10 Do not fear, for I am with you;
>> Do not anxiously look about you, for I am your God.
> I will strengthen you, surely I will help you,
>> Surely I will uphold you with My righteous right hand.
> 13 For I am the Lord your God,
>> who upholds your right hand,
>> Who says to you, "Do not fear, I will help you."

Jesus used the same imagery of the power of God's hand in holding His elect in John 10. Concerning the sheep that the Father had given to Him in eternity past, Jesus said:

> My sheep hear My voice, and I know them, and they follow Me; and I give eternal life to them, and they will never perish; and no one will snatch them out of My hand. My Father, who has given them to Me, is greater than all; and no one is able to snatch them out of the Father's hand. I and the Father are one. (John 10:27-30)

Jesus promised that He would save all those whom the Father gave to Him and raise them up on the last day (John 6:37-44).[6] Not a single one of His sheep shall be lost. God has not only reserved Heaven for us, but He preserves us for Heaven.

1 Peter 1:3–5 says our inheritance is reserved in Heaven and we are being kept by the power of God in order that we not fail

---

6. For a comprehensive exposition of these passages in John, I would encourage you to consult the series of messages I preached during a 7-year study of the gospel. Those messages are archived at the Kootenai Community Church website (http://www.kootenaichurch.org).

to receive the inheritance that Christ has purposed in our salvation. Peter writes:

> Blessed be the God and Father of our Lord Jesus Christ, who according to His great mercy has caused us to be born again to a living hope through the resurrection of Jesus Christ from the dead, to obtain an inheritance which is imperishable and undefiled and will not fade away, reserved in heaven for you, who are protected by the power of God through faith for a salvation ready to be revealed in the last time. (1 Peter 1:3-5)

According to God's counsel, He guides His elect through this life amidst the spiritual perils, dangerous times, potential apostasies, Satan's attacks, and even their own doubts, and brings them safely to glory. As Asaph says, "And afterward receive me to glory" (v. 24).

This is the end of the righteous. We shall enter into His glory. Infinite glory. Eternal glory. We shall behold the glory of God and see the Son, the Captain of our Salvation, in His glory, the glory He had with the Father before the world began (John 17:5). The Great Shepherd of the Sheep shall lead, feed, and protect His flock and bring them all safely to their eternal glory, the glory promised by God long ages ago (Titus 1:2).

Psalm 49:15:
15 But God will redeem my soul from the power of Sheol,
   For He will receive me. Selah.

The wicked shall be forever cut off. Psalm 37:9, 22: "For evildoers will be cut off, but those who wait for the Lord, they will inherit the land. For those blessed by Him will inherit the land, but those cursed by Him will be cut off." God shall never cut off the righteous. The Lord Jesus Christ will never turn them away

(John 6:37). As Jude said, "Now to Him who is able to keep you from stumbling, and to make you stand in the presence of His glory blameless with great joy, to the only God our Savior, through Jesus Christ our Lord, be glory, majesty, dominion and authority, before all time and now and forever. Amen" (Jude 24–25).

He will receive us to glory! Who in their right mind would want to trade places with the wicked?

The Ground of Asaph's Confidence

How could Asaph be so confident? How could he know for sure that God would receive him to glory? The only way Asaph could know this was if he could be absolutely assured of the keeping purposes and power of God for His elect. If it is anything less than the purpose and power of God that keeps His elect unto their final glory, they can have no confidence they shall surely see it.

Asaph could have no confidence in his own ability to persevere to the end. After all, he had just gone through a crisis of faith severe enough to shake the most solid believer to his core. His feet nearly slipped. His steps came close to stumbling. He had started to believe blasphemous things about God and His goodness, reasoning like a fool and a brute beast. This crisis taught Asaph how weak he was in his own strength. He was a prophet of God[7] and a great worship leader under King David, yet his crisis of faith threatened his undoing. If such a great man could ultimately fall to ruin and perish, what hope could you or I possibly have?

If Asaph had believed for one moment that his final perseverance to eternal glory depended on his own strength, he

---

7. 1 Chronicles 25:1-2; 2 Chronicles 29:30.

would never have uttered words such as these: "With Your counsel You will guide me, and afterward receive me to glory." Instead he would have to say, "With my own strength, and by my own effort, I shall hope at last, provided I do not fall again, to make it to eternal glory. I nearly fell once, and I have no confidence at all that I shall not fall again, and this time into eternal ruin and destruction."

Asaph had learned that God's power keeps and preserves those who are His. Though the arm of flesh may fail him, the mighty arm of God that took him by the right hand would bring him safely to glory. If God has purposed the salvation of His people, He shall not fail. He cannot fail. Like Asaph, we can have absolute confidence that He will guide us and receive us safely to glory.

The Goodness of God for Eternity

Psalm 73:25–28

Whom have I in Heaven but You?
And besides You, I desire nothing on earth.
My flesh and my heart may fail,
But God is the strength of my heart
and my portion forever.
For, behold, those who are far from You will perish;
You have destroyed all those who are unfaithful to You.
But as for me, the nearness of God is my good;
I have made the Lord God my refuge,
That I may tell of all Your works.

It is nowhere more evident than here that Asaph's focus has been completely changed. His focus is Heavenward. He expressed confidence that the Lord would receive Him to glory, and now his focus is upon the delights and joys of that glory. His eyes are on the riches of Heaven instead of the riches of the heathen. What a change of perspective has been wrought in Asaph as a result of stepping into the sanctuary of God (v. 17)!

Asaph no longer thought of his lot as being characterized by chastening and affliction (v. 14). He had come to see that God Himself is the treasure and joy of Heaven. God is what makes Heaven Heaven. There is nothing that Heaven can offer which might in any way compare to the treasure to be found in God Himself. Heaven contains no thing and no person as desirable as God. "Whom have I in Heaven but you?" The implied answer to that question is, "Nobody."

All the glitter and gold of this earthly realm had lost its allure. "And besides You, I desire nothing on earth." This stands in stark contrast with his statement in verse 3: "For I was envious of the arrogant as I saw the prosperity of the wicked." He no longer desired their wealth, their prosperity, nor their ease of life. He had come to see God as a treasure far richer, more desirable, and greater by far than anything this earthly realm could offer. His envy of their prosperity came to an end when he saw their end. The prosperity of the wicked is their judgment. The treasure of the righteous is their God. The enticements of luxury and ease had once drawn his heart near to perdition. Rescued by the grace of God from a fall, Asaph found God to be a treasure greater than all that the wicked had or could ever hope to have.

When God was removed from Asaph's view, every lesser light appeared impressive and every earthly enticement began to glitter. But once Asaph's heart fixed upon God, everything lost its luster. What could compare to Him? Who could compare to Him? What is greater, gold or the Creator of gold? What is to be treasured more, the passing riches of this world or the eternal treasure of knowing God?

Psalm 89:6-7:

6 For who in the skies is comparable to the Lord?

Who among the sons of the mighty is like the Lord,

7 A God greatly feared in the council of the holy ones,

And awesome above all those who are around Him?

Great treasures and pleasures, joys and delights await those who shall enjoy the presence of God forever. Psalm 16:11 says, "You will make known to me the path of life; in Your presence is fullness of joy; in Your right hand there are pleasures forever."

If we could only learn this lesson and learn it well. We wake up each morning to a chorus of interests that compete for our affections. The allure of this world is strong and the righteous must fight to make God and God alone their delight and satisfaction. The battle to keep our God as the treasure of our heart and the center of our affections is a real battle that must be fought every day. We must continually ask God to guard us from the idolatry and envy which seeks to steal our affections from Him. No one can be truly happy in this life who does not make God their treasure in this world and their desire in the world to come.

Our Strength and Portion

Asaph had come face to face with his own weakness. He knew his heart was weak. He had come to a point of envying those who are the objects of God's justice. His flesh had deceived him. Only God had preserved him from falling headlong into blasphemy and apostasy. Thus Asaph says, "God is the strength of my heart and my portion forever." If his heart was to remain faithful and focused on the treasure of Heaven, it could only be if God should strengthen his heart. Asaph knew he was weak in his own flesh and his own strength.

When Asaph speaks of God being his "portion forever" he is using "a figurative expression, employed in Scripture to denote the condition or lot with which every man is contented."[8] It described a "share of something, portion, allotment, a part of something, implying it is assigned."[9] The word was used to describe a plot of ground, a small parcel, or a reward. The allotment for the wicked may be gold, fame, and power, but the righteous have God. He is their lot. He is their portion.

Psalm 16:5:

5 The Lord is the portion of my inheritance and my cup;
　　you support my lot.

Psalm 142:5:

5 I cried out to You, O Lord; I said,
　　"You are my refuge, my portion in the land of the living."

This is a particularly comforting truth in difficult and distressing times as Jeremiah learned: "'The Lord is my portion,' says my soul, 'Therefore I have hope in Him'" (Lamentations 3:24).

The riches of this world can never bring contentment and satisfaction. God alone is able to abundantly supply the deepest needs of our soul. Gold will disappoint but God never will. We find "in Him the perfection of our happiness consists."[10] The wise will gladly receive Him as their portion in this life.

---

8. Calvin, 156.
9. J. Swanson, *Dictionary of Biblical Languages with Semantic Domains : Hebrew (Old Testament)* (electronic ed.). Oak Harbor: Logos Research Systems, Inc., 1997.
10. Calvin, 157.

A Final Contrast

The final two verses of the psalm summarize all we have learned thus far. We see a number of final contrasts between the prosperous wicked and the suffering righteous.

Psalm 73:27–28:
27 For, behold, those who are far from You will perish;
You have destroyed all those who are unfaithful to You.
28 But as for me, the nearness of God is my good;
I have made the Lord God my refuge,
That I may tell of all Your works.

Verse 27 describes the agony of the wicked and verse 28 the anthem of the righteous. The wicked are far from God and the righteous are near. The wicked will perish while the righteous enjoy their refuge. The wicked are unfaithful and the righteous faithfully declare the works of God. The wicked refuse to give God glory, the righteous do not. The wicked do not have God, the righteous enjoy His goodness. The wicked will finally forfeit their treasure, the righteous will never have to do so. The wicked get gold in this life; the righteous get God. The wicked lose their gold at death, the righteous keep God. The wicked live this life apart from God and perish in the same state. The righteous draw near to God and their death brings them nearer still. Death for the wicked is eternal separation from the goodness of God. Death for the righteous is an eternal and inseparable nearness to God's goodness.

Though it seemed that Asaph was through speaking of the wicked and their destruction (vv. 18-20), he took up that subject one last time here at the end in order to show by contrast the glorious treasure promised to those whom the Father loves. In the end, the wicked suffer ultimate loss and ruin. They refused to delight themselves in God, to make Him their treasure, and receive His goodness. They loved their wealth, their fame, and their power more than their Creator. They mistakenly thought that the prosperity they enjoyed was a token of either His ignorance or His approval. They could not be more wrong. Their loss could not be more stunning. When they perish, they will suffer the ultimate loss. All they have to live for will dissipate like a dream at dawn. They will enter Hell and suffer for eternity without a single pleasure, joy, or delight. God has promised their destruction: "You have destroyed all those who are unfaithful to You."

The righteous may live their lives here in the most meager of circumstances. They may suffer affliction, persecution and a constant drip of trials, yet, they do and will enjoy a good that defies description – the infinite and eternal God. The nearness of God is their good. The good thing that the righteous enjoys is nothing less than God Himself. The righteous have a prosperity too, but it is not gold. It is God. God is the prosperity of the righteous. That is a prosperity that death cannot take away. It is a prosperity that affliction only makes sweeter and closer. It is a prosperity that the impenitent wicked can never know.

David was surely right when he declared in Psalm 65:4: "How blessed is the one whom You choose and bring near to You to dwell in Your courts. We will be satisfied with the goodness of Your house, Your holy temple."

The righteous enjoy an eternal good. Our delight is an eternal delight, a satisfaction that never ends.

Let Us Declare It!

It is interesting that this psalm ends with Asaph's commitment to declare the gracious works of God: "That I may tell of all Your works" (v. 28). Asaph leaves us with this commission: to declare the vanity of earthly prosperity and the glory of God's merciful goodness. Asaph does this very thing in this psalm. Psalm 73 was written to declare the goodness of God to His people.

Asaph began with that bold declaration in verse 1: "Surely God is good to Israel, to those who are pure in heart!" This psalm is all about that goodness. Asaph has shown that the prosperity of the wicked is not God's goodness to them at all. God is good to those who are His. God is good to His people. Real and lasting goodness is not to be found in wealth and riches, it is found in God. Real blessings are not showered upon rebels but the righteous. The dealings of God among mankind cannot be assessed with the yardstick of time alone. Eternity weighs upon the scales and redefines the terms of that assessment. Let us tell of these marvelous works.

We should not be shy about declaring God's works – all of them. ALL of them. Asaph did not shy away from discussing God's righteous judgments. It was most certainly the work of God to lavish wealth and riches upon the wicked. It was a work of God's judgment. We can and should declare that. God has set His face against the wicked and will use their prosperity to make their punishment more severe and their loss more tragic. That is His work. We should declare that. God's works include the destruction of His enemies and their utter and eternal shame. When they perish, they perish at His hand and He casts them down to destruction. That is His work. We should declare it.

Asaph is not ashamed of these works. God is not ashamed of these works. We should not be ashamed of these works. God works for the glory of His name and the good of His people. Let the redeemed tell of ALL His marvelous works. Let the wicked take heed and call upon Him while they may.

Conclusion

We have learned a lot from Asaph. It is a lesson from an age gone by for the children of God in every age. Every generation needs to hear and learn the lesson of Psalm 73.

Though the names of the prosperous wicked, the styles of their clothing, and their methods of oppressing the righteous may change, the truth of Psalm 73 does not. Every generation of God's people must hear afresh that the riches of this world heaped upon the wicked is not a token of God's favor and blessing. It is a token of a catastrophic judgment to come. This is a lesson for the ages!

In terms of what we have studied in Psalm 73, nothing has changed in the 3,500 years since Asaph penned these words. There is nothing new under the sun. We have studied the words of this psalm mostly focused on the wicked of Asaph's day but it has not been difficult to translate these truths into our own context. It is difficult to study the psalm without immediately thinking of people, businesses, organizations, or nations that fit the descriptions of the prosperous wicked that Asaph gave. There are prosperous wicked in every age - many of them.

In our own day, we have large companies that use their revenues to expand the homosexual agenda, promote and defend the child-killing industry, New Age spirituality, and the oppression of the righteous. Their money is spent to elect politicians who enshrine evil into law and make the oppression of God's people commonplace in our land.

In our own day, we have plenty of prosperous wicked individuals who glorify immorality on screen, in music, and in print. They only increase in wealth. The more they oppose God and oppress His people, the more their wealth and influence grows.

Our own nation has fast become a force for the oppression of truth and opposition to righteousness. We are a land full of people who are more concerned with their comforts than convictions. We are seeing a generation more interested in riches than righteousness and they are willing to pursue unrighteousness if it provides them with the riches. The more the wicked increase in wealth, the more others want to be like them. This is the recipe for an increase in prosperous wicked. Buckle up! We are in for a bumpy ride!

We need to remember the lessons of Psalm 73.

They shall not endure! God intends through their wealth the same thing he intended through the wealth of the wicked in Asaph's day. God's purposes have not changed. His view of prosperity has not changed. His intention to judge the wicked and reward the righteous has not changed. The truth of Psalm 73 has not changed.

I wish to leave you with some words from two other psalms that address the same issues: Psalm 37 and 49.

Psalm 37 deals with the problem of the prosperity of the wicked from a slightly different angle. In Psalm 37 David focuses on God's promises to the righteous in this world without ignoring the blessings of the world to come. He reminds us that God's temporal blessings of provision and posterity properly belong to those who love Him. The wicked flourish for a short time and will be swiftly and suddenly cut off.

Psalm 49 deals with the folly of trusting in riches since both the riches and the pompous wicked who possess them will quickly perish.

Psalm 37:1–7:

1 Do not fret because of evildoers,
   Be not envious toward wrongdoers.
2 For they will wither quickly like the grass
   And fade like the green herb.
3 Trust in the Lord and do good;
   Dwell in the land and cultivate faithfulness.
4 Delight yourself in the Lord;
   And He will give you the desires of your heart.
5 Commit your way to the Lord,
   Trust also in Him, and He will do it.
6 He will bring forth your righteousness as the light
   And your judgment as the noonday.
7 Rest in the Lord and wait patiently for Him;
   Do not fret because of him who prospers in his way,
   Because of the man who carries out wicked schemes.

Psalm 37:38–40:

38 But transgressors will be altogether destroyed;
   The posterity of the wicked will be cut off.
39 But the salvation of the righteous is from the Lord;
   He is their strength in time of trouble.
40 The Lord helps them and delivers them;
   He delivers them from the wicked and saves them,
   Because they take refuge in Him.

Psalm 49:10–12:

10 For he sees that even wise men die;
   The stupid and the senseless alike perish
   And leave their wealth to others.
11 Their inner thought is that their houses are forever
   And their dwelling places to all generations;
   They have called their lands after their own names.
12 But man in his pomp will not endure;
   He is like the beasts that perish.

Psalm 49:16–20:

16 Do not be afraid when a man becomes rich,
   When the glory of his house is increased;
17 For when he dies he will carry nothing away;
   His glory will not descend after him.
18 Though while he lives he congratulates himself -
   And though men praise you when you do
   well for yourself-
19 He shall go to the generation of his fathers;
   They will never see the light.
20 Man in his pomp, yet without understanding,
   Is like the beasts that perish.

Scripture assures us that these wicked will not last. They will be judged. Their wealth is the guarantee of that judgment. It is the first stroke of divine justice. The wicked will wither like a flower and disappear like the dew. The righteous shall endure forever and shine like the sun for all eternity in the glory and felicity of Heaven.

And God will be glorified!

About the Author

Jim Osman was born in May of 1972 and has lived in Sandpoint, Idaho since he was three years old. He graduated from Sandpoint High School in 1990. Jim came to know Christ through the ministry of Cocolalla Lake Bible Camp in the summer of 1987. Kootenai Community Church has always been his home church, attending Sunday School, Vacation Bible School, and Youth Group.

After graduating from High School, Jim attended Millar College of the Bible in Pambrun, Saskatchewan. It was at Bible College that Jim met his wife-to-be, Diedre, who was also enrolled as a student. Jim graduated with a three-year diploma in April of 1993 and married Diedre in August of that same year. He returned to Millar to further his education in September of 1994 and graduated from the Fourth Year Internship Program with a Bachelor of Arts in Strategic Ministries in April of 1995. He was inducted into the Honor Society of the Association of Canadian Bible Colleges and appointed a member of Pi Alpha Mu.

Jim and Diedre returned to Sandpoint where Jim began working in construction as a roofer until he was asked to take over as the preaching elder of Kootenai Community Church in December of 1996. Now he counts it his greatest privilege to be involved in ministering in the church that ministered to him for so many years. He is the author of *Truth or Territory: A Biblical Approach to Spiritual Warfare* and *Selling the Stairway to Heaven: Critiquing the Claims of Heaven Tourists*. You can follow his preaching at the Kootenai Community Church website and his writings at truthorterritory.com.

Jim loves to be outdoors, whether it is camping, hunting, or working in his garden. He enjoys bike riding and watching football, especially his favorite team, the San Francisco 49ers, for whom he has cheered since childhood. Jim and Diedre have four children: Taryn, Shepley, Ayden and Liam. They are all 49er fans!

You can contact Jim through Kootenai Community Church (http://www.kootenaichurch.org) or by writing to him at jimcosman@truthorterritory.com.

Made in the USA
Columbia, SC
18 February 2021

32690363R00117